11 QUESTIONS
GREAT
MANAGERS
ASK & ANSWER

11 QUESTIONS
GREAT
MANAGERS

ASK & ANSWER

TOM GEHRING

ISBN 978-1-7327992-3-3 (hardcover)
ISBN 978-1-7327992-4-0 (paperback)
ISBN 978-1-7327992-5-7 (ebook)

Published by Far Peaks Publishing
San Diego, California
www.farpeaksconsulting.com

For ordering information or special discounts for
bulk purchases or customized editions, please contact
Far Peaks Publishing, (619) 206-8282

Cover and Interior Design and composition
by The Book Designers, www.bookdesigners.com

Publishing Consulting by Karla Olson, BookStudio,
www.bookstudiobooks.com

Printed in the United States of America

DEDICATION

This book is dedicated to five great managers
who taught me so much:
Hyman Rickover, Dick Riddell, Archie Clemins,
Bill Hughes, and Wynn Harding

TABLE OF CONTENTS

FOREWORD

Why did I write this book? Because I believe the most important thing humans do is teach the next generation—and teach them well.

Despite more than forty years of successfully managing everything from nuclear power plants to conventions, I never had a management paradigm. Superb management techniques, yes. An overarching mental model for how to manage, no.

Teaching management to doctors late in my career crystallized four decades of implicit or intuitive concepts about management into a paradigm that I want to pass on to the next generation.

I am neither an academic nor a theoretician. I am a pragmatic practitioner of getting stuff done. I hope you will forgive the lack of intellectual purity and copious academic footnotes, but this paradigm works!

It has been a joy to reflect on my past and to help my readers with their future.

Godspeed, and good luck.

—*Tom Gehring*
San Diego, Spring 2020

INTRODUCTION

Headline Concept – Asking Others

The boss just gave you a big new assignment. Huge opportunity. You are new to management or an inexperienced manager or an experienced manager looking for a unifying theory of management. You are terrified of failure or embarrassment.

You know you can't manage this by doing it all yourself.

You don't know all the answers, and you are not an expert.

What the heck do you do now?

Good news – as a manager, you don't need all the answers – but you do need the right questions.

And you need to be able to tell a wrong answer from the right answer(s).

And you have to be able to find the right answer(s).

An old submarine dictum was that 90 percent (or some largish fraction) of being an effective *manager* was knowing the right question to ask, and the wrong answer.

The first time I heard that, I was incredulous. No, I was flabbergasted. You mean to tell me I was only expected to know the right answer 10 percent (or some smallish fraction)? Seriously?

Yup. But notice the modifier: "as a *manager*."

When you transition from being an expert doer to a manager, you have to give up being the answer-person.

The reason you are reading this book is that you are making the jump from being the answer-person to becoming the question-person – and I'm going to show you how.

Headline Concept – Asking Yourself

You ask others questions you don't necessarily know the answers to.

To make sure you are true to yourself, ask yourself questions for which you likely already know the answer, to help you focus on six personal traits critical to great managers.

Organization of the book

In section 1, I introduce the concept and theory of my Socratic Management Paradigm and lay out the theoretical foundation for its use.

In sections 2, 3, and 4, I describe the eleven core questions of others that form the backbone of the Socratic Management Paradigm. For each of those eleven fundamental questions, I introduce many probing or follow-on questions and then discuss the types of answers that should give you pause.

In section 2, we look at three questions that articulate the problem you are going to solve.

In section 3, we examine six questions that help you define a solution to the problem you identified in section two.

In section 4, we discuss two questions that help you move to a successful conclusion.

In section 5, I present four case studies that will provide context and implementation insights into Socratic Management, and suggest that you, the reader, try your hand at Socratic Management.

In section 6, we examine six traits of great managers that are crucial to Socratic Management.

In appendix 1, I provide some pretty good rules that have helped me manage well.

In appendix 2, I present all the first-order Socratic questions and their associated follow-on questions into one location for easy reference.

Chapter summary

At the end of each chapter, I summarize the key takeaways on a single page, for ease of reproduction and reference.

Chapter lengths

I am not verbose. "Cut to the chase" is one of my favorite sayings, even at home!

Some chapters will be short because, while I want to give the content of the chapter stand-alone recognition, I don't need to say it more than once!

The size of your organization does not matter

The size of the organization is not germane to the Socratic Management Paradigm. Whether you are the CEO of a large organization, running a small family business, or in a workgroup of four, the paradigm and the questions are the same.

Solving = Managing = Being in Charge

I will use three concepts interchangeably: solving a problem, managing a task, and being in charge of a project.

Who did I write this book for?

I wrote this book for all the managers or managers-to-be who are terrified because they don't have a paradigm or process for management.

A final word before we start

Our professional lives have two major phases – the "doer" phase, usually but not always a direct extension of our educational lives, and the "manager" and/or "leader" phase.

In the first life, we are an expert. In our second incarnation, not so much.

As a manager, accept that you are no longer an expert, embrace your supposed "ignorance," and ask lots of smart questions, knowing that you will recognize the wrong answer(s) and that you can find the right answer(s) – and are able, therefore, to manage almost anything.

1

CONCEPT AND THEORY

To become a great manager, you need an underlying theory of management. In chapter 1, I detail the Socratic Management Paradigm.

But no theory lives in a vacuum, so in chapter 2, I set the context for the Socratic Management Paradigm, and specifically connect management and leadership.

Nothing ever works perfectly, so in chapter 3, I describe a number of ways that the Socratic Management Paradigm can fail and outline how to avoid those points of failure.

If you are reading this book, you are likely a perfectionist and insist on (indeed crave) accuracy. In chapter 4, I discuss approximation and accepting imperfection.

Overview of the Socratic Management Paradigm

Every thoughtful manager, sooner or later, will and must ask herself, *How the heck am I going to get this done?*

And while most are taught techniques and tools, very few are taught an overarching management paradigm.

But first, what exactly is a paradigm?

A paradigm is a standard, perspective, or set of ideas. A paradigm is a way of looking at something.

OK, but what is management?

If we need a paradigm for management, we'd better have a definition of management.

There are as many definitions of management as there are managers, but I think it important to this book that I articulate *my* definition.

> **Management is getting something done that would not have been accomplished without you.**

A manager is no longer in the business of personally getting stuff done.

A manager is no longer in the business of personally getting stuff done. A manager is in the business of causing stuff to get done. That's a huge, huge difference.

Why do I need a management paradigm?

Some people are so gifted that management comes to them without any effort. For the rest of us, management is an art and science that is learned and developed over many years.

As an engineer, I believe that process rules. There is a process for almost anything. And central to understanding, building, and modifying processes is a fundamental understanding of the underlying paradigm, model, or theory.

Without that underlying paradigm, model, or theory, a mastery of process gets you nowhere. Paradigm, then process. Paradigm, then technique.

Paradigm, then process. Paradigm, then technique.

And that's why everyone needs a paradigm of management.

Learning management by absorption

As a thirty-year-old, I gained the responsibility for the safe operation and maintenance of a submersible nuclear power plant. Every three or four months, my ship would tie up to a maintenance facility for a four-week upkeep, where my team and the repair facility team would jointly perform preventive and corrective repairs. Think of it as a 60,000-mile checkup on your car, combined with fixing all the brokes that have accumulated since the last visit to the shop.

My German parents gifted me with the organization gene, plus I had served on two maintenance-intensive submarines beforehand.

I was able to (relatively) easily manage the first upkeep, and I got better as I gained experience.

But many years later I reflected that while I was very successful, I was successful because I had mastered the *techniques* of management by absorption, and because of background, experience, and genetics.

But I had no *paradigm* for management.

Asking smart questions

As I grew more experienced as a manager, I learned three fundamental truths about expertise and questions.

First, the more senior you are, the less of an expert you are. Let me illustrate by telling you a bit about my early years.

> **The more senior you are, the less of an expert you are.**

I made the sad mistake of graduating second in my class at the school that prepares you for your first submarine assignment. The guy who graduated first got exactly what he wanted – orders to a super-duper submarine ready for an action-packed deployment into the Soviet backyard[1]. I, on the other hand, was assigned to the oldest (in fact, the first) nuclear submarine, *Nautilus* (SSN-571), doomed to motor never far from our homeport of New London, Conn., with nary a whiff of action against our foes. Our bosses had decreed that only top graduates could go to *Nautilus* since she needed a lot of talent to keep her running. So rather than participate in daring feats of submarining, I was stuck babysitting an engineering nightmare. Woe is me …

Yet I learned so much and served with such a fabulous group of handpicked officers that the experience was (in hindsight) a great one. I left *Nautilus* as a certified wizard on the S1W[2] propulsion plant.

---

1   One of the books in the bibliography, *Blind Man's Bluff*, recounts some of the more adventurous feats pulled off by American submariners during the Cold War – hair-raising stuff of legends. A great read!

2   All submarine reactor plants have a consistent nomenclature – S=submarine, 1=the order of production, and W=Westinghouse, the firm that built the plant.

Only one little problem: I had just become an expert on an antique, an obsolete one-of-a-kind.

I reported to *Pogy* (SSN-647) four years later as Engineer Officer, in charge of an S5W power plant.

S1W vs. S5W, alphabet soup to non-submariners. But it's a critical distinction. An analogy is helpful. Think of me as a mechanic who apprenticed on a Model-T Ford and then became lead mechanic on a Formula 1 race car. Same basic principles, same basic construction, completely different implementation – three generations more modern. I was certainly not an expert on *that particular* propulsion plant.

Second, the more experienced you are, the better you are at asking questions.

> **The more experienced you are, the better you are at asking questions.**

Before *Pogy*, I had served almost four years at sea on two older submarines and had spent two years as a Maintenance Officer at a submarine squadron.

I had been taught by my seniors, peers, and subordinates to ask really good questions.

I got better and better at asking penetrating questions even though I did not necessarily possess expertise in that particular area.

Third, the more you've seen, the better you are at sensing the wrong answer (even though you're not an expert).

> **The more you've seen, the better you are at sensing the wrong answer.**

After almost four years as Engineer Officer of *Pogy*, I was assigned as the Squadron Engineer, where I was responsible for the upkeep and maintenance of ten of the oldest submarines in the Navy. Continuing the automobile analogy, I was now in charge of a garage full of oldish and highly temperamental 1950s race cars.

We dealt with the most challenging of technical problems. My boss, Commodore Bill Hughes, had likewise served on older submarines and had a tremendous breadth of experience.

One day, we had an intractable problem with a large valve associated with the diesel engine[3]. After my teams wrestled unsuccessfully with this problem for a couple of days, Commodore Hughes asked me to bring the technical drawings up to his cabin and explain the situation to him. After five minutes of his insightful questions, I discovered where my team and the team from the maintenance facility had been going wrong. Pure magic, we thought. Not really. The Commodore had sensed, based on his long experience, that the answers he was getting to his questions were wrong, and he (tactfully) pointed out the error of our ways!

The Socratic Method

Webster's New World College Dictionary, Fifth Edition, defines the Socratic method as "a pedagogical technique in which a teacher does not give information directly but instead asks a series of questions, with the result that the student comes either to the desired knowledge by answering the questions or to a deeper awareness of the limits of knowledge."

One online source defines the Socratic method as "a form of cooperative argumentative dialogue between individuals, based on asking and answering questions to stimulate critical thinking and to draw out ideas and underlying presuppositions."

The 1973 movie, *The Paper Chase*, tells the story of a first-year student at Harvard Law School who is bedeviled by the dreaded Professor Kingsfield. Using the Socratic, rather than the didactic method[4], Kingsfield acerbically challenges his students with questions demanding knowledge of the case *and* the ability to think on their feet. The professor does not tell them the answer, rather he leads the students to the conclusion. And sometimes there is more than one conclusion.

---

3   Nuclear submarines have a large diesel engine as an alternative power source to the nuclear reactor.

4   In the didactic method, the teacher gives instructions to the students and the students are mostly passive listeners and notetakers.

In simple terms, the Socratic method is about asking great questions to allow the student to arrive at the answer.

The Socratic Management Paradigm

After decades of successful management and years of teaching management *techniques* to doctors, I finally came up with a model for management that I dubbed the "Socratic Management Paradigm."

The Socratic Management Paradigm applies the principles of "asking and answering questions to stimulate critical thinking and to draw out ideas and underlying presuppositions" to management by identifying eleven essential questions that great managers must be able to ask of their team (if they are managing down) and answer to their boss (if they are managing up).

The eleven questions

Journalism majors are taught "Don't bury the lead." So here it is!

While there is a nearly limitless supply of questions that a manager can ask, the Socratic Management Paradigm starts by asking eleven fundamental questions in three broad areas: problem definition, solution generation, and solution implementation.

To define the problem, ask:

1. *What is the problem* we are trying to solve?
2. *Why* are we solving that problem?
3. *For whom* are we solving that problem?

To generate a solution, ask:

4. *How* are we going to solve the problem?
5. *Who* is going to do what?
6. *Where* are we doing what?
7. *When* are we doing what?
8. *How long* will it take?
9. *How much* will it cost?

To implement the solution, ask:

    10. How will we *monitor* the plan?

    11. How will we *learn and improve*?

No stone tablets

There is nothing magical or absolute about my eleven questions. After reading the detailed explanation in the following sections, I encourage you to add to, modify, or subtract from this list of questions.

Probing

The eleven questions are not the end but rather the beginning.

It is critical to developing your management skills that you learn to probe. Tactfully, (mostly) gently, but inexorably.

> **The eleven questions are not the end but rather the beginning.**

For each chapter in section 2, I will suggest many follow-on questions.

As you gain in managerial experience, you will add your own techniques to probe and teach further.

Your sense of (figurative) smell

The smell on a submarine is distinctive and overpowering, and not one created by Coco Chanel!

When I came home from sea, even from short periods, my wife would suggest (strongly) that perhaps all my clothes should go straight to the washer (or the trash can, as long as it was outside our house), and that an immediate lengthy shower would be in order.

Yet despite this olfactory assault, submariners learn quickly that a sense of smell is an important tool.

Electrical problems in particular often announce themselves with an unmistakable acrid odor. On more than one occasion, I shortstopped a potentially lethal casualty by literally following my nose.

Likewise, with management. You need to follow your sense of smell. Not literally, but figuratively.

If the answer to your question feels wrong, smells of (figurative) excrement, then you should follow your instincts and probe deeper. Much deeper. Much, much deeper!

Just like Commodore Hughes in the story of the diesel valve repairs that were not going well, who sensed/smelled that we were headed in the wrong direction, and pointed us down the right road!

Wrong answer! Now what?

So your senses and experience are telling you the answer presented to you is wrong.

Now what? How do you get to the right answer(s)?

There are, in today's information-rich environment, a plethora of sources.

> **If the answer to your question feels wrong, follow your instincts and probe much, much deeper!**

Show me the reference

The first, and often overlooked, answer is the tech manual (or the rules or the written guidance or whatever documentation exists).

I continue to be amazed at how often the answer is hiding in plain sight – in the relevant documents.

One of my favorite questions, when presented with an apparently wrong answer, is "What does the documentation say?" Often, no one has looked because of something known as "tribal knowledge."

In many organizations, expertise is passed on from one generation to the next by word of mouth. Regretfully, humans being fallible, sometimes (actually, often) the pass-down process adds errors, and the "experts" have it wrong – but no one questions them because they are the "experts."

> **Often the answer is hiding in plain sight.**

So when your nose twitches at a potentially wrong answer, have them bring you the reference!

But there is no readily available reference
Anything on the internet must be taken with a grain of salt. But it's not a bad place to start if there is no documentation.

Querying social media or the innumerable bulletin boards is more risky, as it makes it clear that you (and you cannot hide your identity on social media, no matter what anyone tells you) have a problem.

Books and reputable journals are usually a more robust source. I often leapfrog from the internet to books/journals.

But the best place to start is your network of peers and mentors.

There is an important presumption: that you have a network. It is so important to have a sizable group of peers and mentors in place before you need them.

Finally, rent an expert. There is so much talent out there – the trick is not so much to find expertise as to choose it.

And don't limit yourself to external expertise. For any medium to large organization, there are probably in-house experts who can help you toward the right answer. But, as with any in-house talent, there is probably a lack of confidentiality, so proceed with caution.

Odds are you are probably not the first person who has ever run into this particular problem/question. So survey your peers and your mentors, ask for someone who has had a similar problem/question, and see what they say.

There is usually not just one answer
It's easy to be seduced by the first (and sometimes loudest) answer.

The more experienced the manager, the more care she takes in accepting the first (or the first few) answers presented to her questions.

It's easy to be seduced by the first (and sometimes loudest) answer.

The citizens of Missouri have it right with their state motto: "Show me." It's a great attitude for a manager.

CHAPTER SUMMARY

- Management is getting something done that would not have been accomplished without you.
- A paradigm is a standard, perspective, or set of ideas. A paradigm is a way of looking at something.
- The Socratic Management Paradigm applies the principles of "asking and answering questions to stimulate critical thinking and to draw out ideas and underlying presuppositions" to management by identifying eleven essential questions that great managers must be able to ask and answer.
- The more experienced you are, the less expertise you have but the better you are at asking questions and at sensing the wrong answer.
- The Socratic Management Paradigm focuses on eleven core questions:

    To define the problem, ask:
    - ✓ *What is the problem* we are trying to solve?
    - ✓ *Why* are we solving that problem?
    - ✓ *For whom* are we solving that problem?

    To generate a solution, ask:
    - ✓ *How* are we going to solve the problem?
    - ✓ *Who* is going to do what?
    - ✓ *Where* are we doing what?
    - ✓ *When* are we doing what?
    - ✓ *How long* will it take?
    - ✓ *How much* will it cost?

    To implement the solution, ask:
    - ✓ How will we *monitor* the plan?
    - ✓ How will we *learn and improve*?

- The eleven questions are not the end, but rather the beginning.

- If you know that the answer to your question(s) is (are) wrong, find the right answer(s) by:
  - ✓ Checking the reference (or documentation).
  - ✓ Checking the internet.
  - ✓ Checking the (virtual) library (quaint ... and surprisingly effective since most print media has been digitized).
  - ✓ Checking with your peers and network.
  - ✓ Renting an expert.
- Don't jump to the first (or loudest) answer. Have them "show you."

Setting the Context for the Management Paradigm

2

Doing and doers

Most of us learn, early in our professional lives, a skill, a trade, or a body of knowledge that allows us to accomplish stuff.

I learned about submarining and nuclear power so that when I walked onboard my first ship, I was quickly productive in the realm of "doing."

My wife went to medical school and completed an internship and a residency so that she was an effective psychiatric clinician immediately after her training.

We were both trained as "doers."

> In the world of doing, you are expected to know the right answer(s).

In the world of doing, you are expected to know the right answer(s).

Perhaps not 100 percent of the time, but pretty darn close.

You really don't want the surgeon performing your appendectomy guessing as to which side the appendix is on. Likewise, if you are starting up the nuclear reactor, improvising is not a good option.

You are not a "doer" anymore

But as you gain in seniority, and you assume the mantles of leadership and/or management, you are no longer a "doer."

It is helpful (but sometimes, actually not) to know a lot about what you are leading or managing.

But in the world of leading and managing, you are not expected to be a technical expert.

> **In the world of leading and managing, you are not expected to be a technical expert.**

What is the difference between leadership and management?

Leadership and management are often used in the same sentence and are often conflated.

In my first book, *7 Roles Great Leaders Don't Delegate*, I proposed that leadership was "taking a group of people to a place they would not have gotten to without you."

I suggested that leaders have seven unique roles: sensing, visioning, acculturation, enabling, deciding, embracing responsibility, and mentoring.

Management is not leadership. Related, often done at the same time, often by the same person, but different.

> **Management is not leadership. Leadership is not management.**

In chapter 1, I defined management as "getting something done that would not have gotten done without you."

Peter Drucker stated that leadership is doing the right things, and management is doing things right.

Using a railroad analogy, leadership is about deciding the destinations for the train lines, and management is about laying the track and then making sure the trains run on time.

Why does the distinction matter?

You cannot approach the role of management using your leadership skills. Likewise, you cannot lead using your management skills.

For a given situation, you have to decide whether to use a paradigm for leadership or a paradigm for management. Same person, different process.

And often, you have to use both paradigms at the same time.

We have all met great leaders who are poor managers and vice versa.

The key is to be great at both. And that's why I wrote *both* books.

Managing down vs. managing up

I titled this book *11 Questions Great Managers Ask & Answer* to emphasize the duality of management.

The normal perspective is that you are managing a group of people who report to you – your team. The colloquialism is that you are "managing down."

Likewise, if you report to someone and are working to make that person successful, then you would likely be "managing up."

If you are managing down, then you get to ask the questions.

If you are, however, managing up, then you would be expected to know the answers. But if your boss is an effective manager, then his questions would not be dissimilar to the questions you would ask. Therefore, it behooves you to know the answers to the expected questions for your span of control.

Simply put: Ask the questions to your reports and be able to answer the questions from your boss.

Ask the questions to your reports and be able to answer the questions from your boss.

Ninety percent of management is knowing the right questions to ask - and the wrong answers

I introduced this fundamental and mind-bending concept earlier.

You probably still have the same response: "Come on, Mr. Gehring, surely you jest! I'm the boss – I must know more than my team!"

Maybe. But maybe not.

In this extraordinarily complicated world, you cannot know it all. And very shortly after you stop being a "doer," your technical expertise decays quickly.

Sometimes we can't even keep up from one revision of a computer operating system to the next – never mind getting your smartphone to behave.

So, you have two choices. One is spending twenty-six hours of every day keeping up your knowledge of the details – and

> **Embrace that you don't know nearly as much as you used to.**

forgoing sleep, a life, and your real job as a manager.

Or you can embrace the fact that you don't know nearly as much as you used to, and appreciate that you are now much better at asking questions than coming up with answers.

On my first ship, the previously mentioned *Nautilus*, all officers were required to stand watch in the propulsion plant – irrespective of seniority.

The youngsters, myself included, were serious experts because we were required to be and because we had no experience. In fact, we made up for our lack of experience with deep knowledge. The older officers were not experts, but they knew the essentials and the principles and had the experience and systems knowledge to ask questions for the rest.

From this dichotomy, I came to the idea that 90 percent of being an effective manager is knowing the right questions to ask and the wrong answers.

> **90 percent of being an effective manager is knowing the right questions to ask and the wrong answers.**

Some caveats:

- The percentages (90 and 10) are completely arbitrary numbers – it's really a smallish or largish fraction of the universe of knowledge in your world. Your actual mileage may differ!
- For some smallish fraction of your managerial universe, you need to know the right questions *and* the right answers.
- One of the keys to being an effective manager (or leader) is knowing what requires you to be an expert. Said differently, pick your 10 percent.

About that 10 percent...

So exactly what are you going to be the expert on? For which 10 percent of your universe will you be the go-to person?

It depends.

When I was a senior consultant at Booz|Allen|Hamilton, I worked with many high-tech organizations. In almost every case, I had no clue about the fine-grain (or even large-grain) details of their business and technical models. But I knew how to do strategic planning and visioning. That's why they brought me to the table. That was my 10 percent.

A submarine is a warship, and although waving the flag (only while surfaced!) and going to exotic foreign ports was fun, our fundamental mission was to sink the enemy in time of war. And the warfighting expertise resided in the Captain and his small team of officers. This cadre had to be *bona fide* experts on the tactics and operation of this multibillion-dollar weapons platform. No one wanted the officers to guess or shrug their shoulders or be clueless at battle stations. That was my 10 percent.

So think deeply about what in your universe you must (or choose to) be an expert on.

> **Think deeply about what you must (or choose to) be an expert on.**

CHAPTER SUMMARY

- In the world of doing, you are expected to know the right technical answer.
- In the world of leading or managing, you are not expected to be a technical expert.
- Management is not leadership. Related, often done at the same time, but different.
- You cannot approach the role of management using your leadership skills. Likewise, you cannot lead using your management skills.
- If you are managing down, then you ask the questions.
- If you are managing up, then you would be expected to know the answers.
- Embrace that you don't know nearly as much as you used to.
- Appreciate that you are much better at asking questions than coming up with answers.
- Ninety percent (or so) of being an effective manager is knowing the right questions to ask, the wrong answer(s), and where to find the right answer.
- Know what 10 percent (or so) of your universe you have to be an expert on.

What Could Possibly Go Wrong with the Socratic Management Paradigm?

Now that I've described the Socratic Management Paradigm, let's do a pre-mortem to see what could possibly go wrong with the system.

What's a pre-mortem?

Everyone is familiar with a post-mortem. When things go wrong, this is where fingers are pointed, voices are raised, blame is assigned (often to the innocent), etc ...

The concept of a pre-mortem was developed to brainstorm anything and everything that could possibly go wrong *before failure*, and then to take proactive steps to preclude failure.[5]

Problem #1: There is no expertise

I reported to my second submarine, *Haddo* (SSN-604), in 1980 at the end of the post-Vietnam military debacle. As the Weapons Officer, I was responsible for the sonar, the torpedoes, and the

---

5   The Pre-Mortem: A Simple Technique To Save Any Project From Failure, https://www.riskology.co/pre-mortem-technique/

fire control systems. And we were going to deploy to the front lines (the Indian Ocean during the Iran hostage crisis) six months after I reported aboard.

As on many older submarines at the end of the '70s, much was broken or in poor shape because our nation had not spent adequate maintenance dollars for a decade. Not surprisingly, the combination of very high operational tempo and low maintenance dollars caused the material condition of the fleet to deteriorate.

Just to make it really interesting, many of the talented sailors who had joined the submarine force to avoid the rice paddies of Vietnam had left the service and rejoined the civilian community.

My management problem was gargantuan.

And I had no experts. They had left the Navy. And much was broken or breaking.

So the mantra "Ninety percent of management is knowing the right question to ask and the wrong answer" works if your people have the expertise and they do know the right answer. But what if they don't? What if your team is truly clueless?

The first six months were really painful, as was the following six-month deployment. I realized that I had to quickly (really, really quickly) become the expert because there was no one to fall back on.

I looked everything up. I checked everything myself. I, by necessity, had to become a micromanager.

I did not sleep much. It was not fun.

In the civilian world, we would have paid for a crew of high-priced consultants to bring expertise to the table. Or we would have quickly hired the expertise. But sometimes you do not have that option.

Your team might not know the answers.

So be very attuned to the real-world possibility that your team really does not know the answers.

Problem #2: Your boss fails you

What happens if there is a failure of leadership? Let's say your boss assigns you a task that makes no sense. Or the project is clearly impossible: under-resourced, over-tasked, Dilbertian[6]. Short of a Herculean effort or divine intervention, this task is not going to get done successfully. What do you do?

A well-known illustration was the Charge of the Light Brigade during the Crimean War in the nineteenth century. More than 600 British cavalrymen were, through a series of inadvertent and malicious miscommunications, ordered to attack a heavily de-fended and impenetrable target. The order, as presented to the leader of the Light Brigade, was clearly nuts. But, they charged into the Valley of Death anyway. The results were predictable and tragic – the brigade was eviscerated.

Alfred, Lord Tennyson memorialized their courage in his eponymous poem but failed to point out the insanity of following a crazy, stupid order.

You will find yourself, at some point in the future, in such a position.

A superbly managed task in a fatally flawed environment rarely succeeds.

So, if your leadership fails you, stop.

Regretfully, your options at that point are not pretty.

> **A superbly managed task in a fatally flawed environment rarely succeeds.**

- ✓ Option 1: You can proceed after making your concerns very public. And you, like the British cavalrymen, are likely doomed.
- ✓ Option 2: If you can resign/depart, do so. Not a great option, but consider the alternative.

---

6   Referring to the comic strip character whose boss is a combination of moron and sociopath. Dilbert's boss repeatedly assigns him work designed to fail – and it does!

When I was second in command (Executive Officer or XO) of *Gurnard* (SSN-662), we were operating near Vancouver, Canada, in December (hint – it was very, very cold and nasty, nasty rough). We were surfaced and scheduled to disembark several tech reps to a small boat that was to come alongside a slippery, icy, and curved deck in a heavy sea. As XO, I was to supervise the offload. I had deep misgivings, but because of perceived operational necessity (an excuse that would have vaporized at the courts-martial had we killed someone), I acceded to my Captain's order.

Dumb. Seriously dumb.

Luckily, no one was hurt.

I was so shaken about my bad decision that I resolved, in private with the Captain, never to accede to a dumb order again, even if it meant losing my job.

Sometimes you have to say no.

Problem #3: Heroic effort will be required

Yet, there may come a time where you are asked to manage a task that, under normal circumstances, you would never take on.

It's a task that, on the surface, is "really dumb."

However, and this requires excruciatingly delicate judgment, there may come a time where you have to take risks. Big risks. But deliberate risks.

Consider the example of *Gurnard* offloading personnel in icy and rough conditions. Now change the circumstances – say it was wartime, and we had to offload the same people under the same horrid conditions, but they were carrying intelligence that absolutely had to be brought ashore.

I would have accepted much more risk, and would have made a completely different call!

The trick is to know the difference between normal and exceptional circumstances and how (and why) the rules change.

Problem #4: Not listening to the critics

There is a corollary to the example of the Charge of the Light Brigade.

If you are in charge, and the little voice in your head says, *This is really dumb*, then stop. I will expand on listening to your inner voice in chapter 23.

Know the difference between normal and exceptional circumstances and how (and why) the rules change.

If you are in charge, and one of your team tells you, "This is dumb," be extraordinarily careful not to dismiss said concern out of hand.

And if your people have the courage to tell you that something you are doing makes no sense, praise them and thank them.

If you are in charge, and the little voice in your head says, "*This is really dumb*," STOP.

Another story from days at sea. Toward the end of my time running the nuclear power plant on *Pogy*, I developed a potentially disastrous malady – I became convinced of my own infallibility. During our final nuclear safety exam, we had scored the best of any submarine in the Pacific Fleet, obviously due to my brilliant leadership and management. Or so I thought.

I made it a habit to give responsibility to my sailors, irrespective of seniority, based only on merit.

My youngest enlisted supervisor and I were closing out the reactor compartment[7] and I insisted, forcefully, that something

---

7   One of the last steps before starting up the nuclear reactor is a supervisory walk-through of the space that houses the reactor core, to make sure there are no problems. Radiation levels in the rest of the plant are quite low, but once critical, radiation levels inside the locked and shielded reactor compartment are lethal. So getting the final walk-through perfect was very important, as there is no entering the compartment once criticality is achieved, and you have to live with any problem you didn't find and correct during the walk-through.

needed to be done (the details don't matter now, and frankly, I forget the specifics).

What I do clearly remember was him telling me I was wrong. Dead wrong. Forcefully. Using extremely colorful language. His finger (literally) in my chest.

That took a lot of guts on his part because of the extreme mismatch in rank and age.

Not to be outdone, I responded in kind – for about five seconds. And then I had a life-changing epiphany.

If your people are willing to stick their necks out to tell you that you are making a big mistake, don't "shoot the messenger." Instead, encourage the messenger, listen to the messenger, promote the messenger. The career you save may be your own!

> **If your people are willing to stick their necks out to tell you that you are making a big mistake, don't "shoot the messenger."**

Needless to say, he was right, I was wrong, and we did it his way – the correct way.

Problem #5: (Under) Resourcing

The most common problem in managing under poor leadership is under-resourcing.

Work extra hours – sure. Work with antiquated equipment – no problem. Put up with bad teammates – hey, we're "can-do."

As a leader, not as a manager, your job is to make sure that you have enabled the manager by providing the right tools - culture, people, money, priorities, tools, and knowledge - to your managers.

If you are both the leader and the manager, then it's on you to enable your team.

As a manager, your job is to highlight the lack of tools, and, absent an existential task, stop.

If you don't give your people – or cause them to receive – what they need to be successful, you are simply emulating that horrid boss in Dilbert.

As a manager, your job is to highlight the lack of tools, and, absent an existential task, stop.

CHAPTER SUMMARY

- Learn the technique of pre-mortem, where you look for, and correct, all the things that could go wrong before starting.
- Problem #1: Be attuned to the real-world possibility that your team really does not know the answers.
- Problem #2: A superbly managed task in a fatally flawed environment is rarely a success. So, if leadership fails or if vision is lacking, stop.
- Problem #3: Sometimes, even when you know the environment is truly challenging, you have to take risks and manage the "impossible."
    - ✓ Know the difference between normal and emergency circumstances, and how the rules change.
- Problem #4: Listen to the voices of your team.
- Problem #5: If your team does not have the culture, people, money, priorities, tools, and knowledge to be successful – stop and resolve the under-resourcing.

In Praise of Approximation

4

Another difficult transition from "doer" to "manager" deals with approximation, or in the vernacular, "guesstimation."

Good enough, not perfect

As a "doer," you were usually, but not always, expected to know the answer precisely. At a minimum, you were expected to know the range of accuracy.

But in your new world of management, you must become comfortable with not knowing the answer precisely.

> **You must become comfortable with not knowing the answer precisely.**

In World War Two, the submarine force used torpedoes that went (usually) [8] where they were told to go. Because the torpedoes were not "smart," i.e., they did what you told them to and no more, the submariner had to know, *precisely*, the course, speed, and range of the target to assure a satisfactory weapons

---

[8] In the first eighteen months of the submarine war in the Pacific, American torpedoes had a nasty habit of not going where they were told, and even if they did, not exploding when they should. And on more than one occasion, they turned on the launching submarine and blew it out of the water.

geometry. As a result, skippers had to get uncomfortably close to their targets to obtain the very accurate solution necessary for a hit.

Fast-forward to the Cold War. Our torpedoes had become extremely smart. Simplifying, you pointed the torpedo in the general direction of the target, and the torpedo (usually) found the target on its own. Your solution did not need to be anywhere near as accurate as for a World War Two torpedo.

Yet institutional memories were long. The more accurate your solution, the "better" you were as a skipper. But you didn't need to be that accurate. In fact, you stood your submarine into danger by getting too close to the target.

We had to retrain a generation of shooters to accept a solution as "good enough" (and not "perfect") for the new torpedoes.

The same principle applies to management. You have to think about when close enough is good enough. Perfection truly is the enemy of (most) progress.

> **Perfection is the enemy of (most) progress.**

Seduction by gizmo

We have become addicted to our electronic gizmos for two reasons: our devices are extremely accurate, and they are extremely convenient.

That leads to several problems.

GIGO

A well-known acronym in computer science is Garbage In Garbage Out (GIGO).

So, while our devices are fast and convenient, inaccurate input will give you a very precise and totally inaccurate output. Just because the answer is displayed to eight significant digits does not mean it is correct!

Question the inputs. Ask where they came from and what the basis for the inputs was.

> **Question the inputs.**

What, no computers?

The second problem deals with reliability. What happens when the internet goes down or your gizmo runs out of juice?

Usually, everything grinds to a halt.

Nautilus, the world's first nuclear submarine, had a World War Two system to determine the target's course, speed and range. We would joke that if you told the system where the target was, it would add error, and then tell you where the target wasn't. Not particularly useful for chasing down sophisticated Cold War targets. But we still had our brains, our slide rules, and pencil/paper. So, the sailors and officers got to be pretty good at solving problems in the absence of the cool gizmos on more modern submarines.

Fast-forward to my third ship, which had every bell and whistle possible. We were able to work wonders with a brilliant team and state-of-the-art machines. One day at battle stations on *Pogy*, I had an epiphany. What if our gizmos, which we had become very adept at operating, stopped? After all, if we went in harm's way, battle damage was a real possibility.

So I simulated that our state-of-the-art machines stopped working.

The result was eye-popping. My incredibly smart and well-trained team simply stopped. Frozen. Hands in laps – literally. After all, no gizmo, no solution.

That's when I became a believer in training both with and without the machines.

> **Train both with and without the machines.**

We taught the *Pogy* team, with the cool gizmos, to use the *Nautilus* pencil/paper/slide-rule techniques. And interestingly, we became much much better when we used both modalities, because the pencil/paper/slide-rule techniques created an independent second solution.

If our pencil/paper/slide-rule solution and the gizmo solution independently converged, we knew we were good. And if the computers suddenly stopped, we had a viable backup plan.

So, as a manager, what's your plan if the gizmos stop? After all, the internet is always accessible, electrical power is on 100.0 percent of the time, and accidents never happen ... Yeah, right!

What could possibly go wrong with this gizmo?

One of my favorite questions, "What could possibly go wrong here?" will help you address all those "It could never happen here!" events.

"What could possibly go wrong here?" is a great way to kick off the pre-mortem mentioned in chapter 3.

What could possibly go wrong here?

As CEO of an association of 3,000 doctors, I lived (and perished) by our member database. Without the database, we could not bill (i.e., no revenue), we could not communicate with our customers (i.e., unhappy or clueless member physicians), and we could not engage our doctors in the vital tasks of advocacy (i.e., no influence). All data was located (at first) on one desktop computer in one office. We were way too close to the precipice.

In 2007, during the massive wildfires in San Diego, I drove through flying embers and apocalyptic fire conditions to rescue that one desktop in that one office. The database safely liberated, we immediately got way smarter – backups layered on top of backups – in the cloud, in remote locations, on thumb drives, etc. That database was never going to be threatened again, ever.

What amazes me, in hindsight, was that I, a technically proficient executive, had not thought to ask and probe, "What could possibly go wrong here?"

Oh, and just in case everything failed, including the electricity, we kept a paper printout of the database in a fireproof safe. Belt and suspenders!

Do the math in your head!

I've sat in many a presentation where a senior, highly experienced manager will look at a slide, and after mere seconds, point out a math error or an incorrect calculational assumption.

Everyone in the room silently wonders, *How the heck did she figure that out?* And the slide had only been displayed for seconds.

The answer is simple – experience plus habit.

These senior leaders have a lot of experience, and so when an answer or number looks wrong, their internal alarm bells go off.

But more importantly, like these apparent magicians, you must teach yourself to become adept at quick mental math.

Hyman Rickover, the creator of the world's first nuclear power plant (which happened to submerge), was adamant about his team knowing how to look at a situation and approximate an answer – quickly.

We even had a name for it: RADCON math (which stood for Radiological Control mathematics). It originated from the need to quickly assess the impact and implications of radiological situations without an electronic calculator or a slide rule (yesterday's calculator).[9]

When presented with a simulated casualty, officers and crew were expected to calculate the expected values of radiological parameters. Quickly. In their heads. Rough orders of magnitude, not precise answers.

In addition to then taking action concomitant with the calculated values, operators were trained to look for nonconforming data. For example, if your radiation monitor displayed a value 100 times what you expected based on your RADCON math, something was wrong – either the instrument had failed or your problem was much bigger than you thought.

---

9   Baby Boomers and members of the Greatest Generation grew up using a calculator that never needed a charger, never required an operating system update, and did not require an internet connection – the aforementioned slide rule! Quaint, quick, accurate *enough*, and totally reliable.

While the original technique was designed for one specific application, it quickly became apparent that the discipline was applicable to almost everything where a quick and rough calculation would be helpful.

Learn to do the math in your head!

Learn to do math in your head!

Imperfection is OK

If you are a manager, you probably have a virulent strain of Type A in your genome. You expect precision. You want the right answer, quickly. You hate messy. You demand perfection – most of all from yourself.

Get over it.

Great managers are constantly, but consciously, trading time and effort for accuracy and perfection. The longer you take and the more effort you expend, the more likely your solution will approach perfection. But you don't have an infinite supply of time and energy. So the level of accuracy in the solution has to be a choice made by the manager.

If you demand perfection all the time, your progress will be slow, if at all. Learn to accept imperfection.

The accuracy of the solution is a choice.

Think of a periodic conversation with your Chief Financial Officer (CFO). How accurate do *you* really have to be? The accountant or the micromanager in you will want to balance to the penny. Your CFO will want to balance to the penny. You, the CEO, don't have the time.

If you have a six-figure budget, worry about the six-figure numbers, the five-figure numbers, and (maybe) the four-figure numbers. Ignore the rest.

It's fine (usually) for your CFO to obsess to the penny, but spend *your* CEO time on what really matters, not minutiae.

CHAPTER SUMMARY

- Become comfortable with not knowing the answer precisely.
- Inaccurate input will give you a very precise and totally inaccurate output.
- Question inputs.
- Prepare for when the internet goes down or your gizmo runs out of juice.
- Teach yourself to become adept at quick mental math.
- If you demand perfection all the time, your progress will be slow, if at all.

THE THREE QUESTIONS THAT DEFINE THE PROBLEM

The Socratic Management Paradigm is designed around three phases of a problem. First, define the problem. Second, create a solution to that problem. Third, implement that solution and determine whether the solution is effective.

In this section, I ask three first-order questions designed to help you clearly articulate the problem you are trying to solve:

1. What's the problem?
2. Why does it need to be solved?
3. Whom are we solving it for?

There are many second-order questions, but they all combine to achieve a clarity of task that your customers, your stakeholder(s), and most importantly, your team, can understand.

Absent clarity here, any attempt at a solution is not likely to succeed. Quoting Lewis Carroll in *Alice in Wonderland*, "If you don't know where you're going, any road will get you there!"

State the Problem

Socratic Question #1: What is the problem we are trying to solve?
State the problem you are trying to solve.

It seems so obvious as to not even be worthy of a question. Next chapter, please.

Not so fast. I have seen too many examples of problem definitions, large and small, that have no clarity.

Ask yourself how many times, as a loyal team member, you've caught yourself scratching your head and asking, "What are we doing here?" or "What are we really trying to accomplish?"

So, read on!

If you don't know where you're going, any road will get you there
The task or project must solve a clearly stated and easily understood problem.

Consider the engineers laboring to put together the giant Saturn V rockets used to lift the Apollo spacecraft into Earth orbit half a century ago.

What was the problem they were trying to solve? At the detail level, it could be a thousand micro-tasks. At the strategic level, simple: "Create the lift vehicle to achieve Earth orbit to put a man on the moon in this decade."[10] Everyone understood, and everyone was pulling in that direction.

> **The task or project must solve a clearly stated and easily understood problem.**

Writing a problem statement precedes all other steps

I heard myself say many times in my younger days, "I don't have time for this touchy-feely stuff of writing a problem statement. Have to get moving! I know what we have to do. I know all the myriad tasks that I have to start or delegate."

No, wait!

Take a deep breath if you find yourself getting impatient before starting on a problem or task. Spend the time upfront to decide on and articulate what problem you are trying to solve.

I love to hike and backpack. On more than one occasion, in my impatience, I've started at the wrong trailhead, and promptly found myself either lost or far down the wrong trail. Often annoying, and potentially life-threatening.

So, take the time to pick the right trail – it will save you much time and effort.

KISS

Keep it (the problem statement) simple and short. [11]

> **Keep the problem statement simple and short.**

Once you've drafted an overarching problem statement, then you can (and must) add layers of complexity – but that's part of the creation of the plan, not the problem statement.

---

10   John F. Kennedy before Congress on May 25, 1961, proposed that the US "should commit itself to achieving the goal, before this decade is out, of landing a man on the Moon and returning him safely to the Earth."

11   Traditionally, KISS stands for "Keep It Simple, Stupid," which I intensely dislike because it's both derogatory and inadequate. For me, KISS stands for "Keep It Simple and Short"

If everyone on the team, and I do mean everyone, knows the problem you are trying to solve, you are much more likely to be successful.

Having a clear problem statement is (obviously) not enough

It is perhaps obvious, but it bears stating. Clearly articulating a problem doesn't mean you have automatically created a solution.

But it's unlikely that you'll get to a solution or a plan without a clear statement of the problem.

Beware of solutions masquerading as problem statements

Many managers are tempted into a solution set disguised as a problem statement by well-meaning, even passionate, stakeholders, customers, or even team members.

As a woodworker, I am enthralled by the latest cool tools. But there is an adage that says "customers want a ¼ inch hole, not necessarily a ¼ inch drill bit." So, my woodworking problem statement should read "I need a ¼" hole at this location," not "I need to purchase a titanium ¼" Forstner bit for this location."

Be particularly cautious about enthusiastic customers or stakeholders driving a problem statement toward a *specific solution* set.

Probing Question #1-A: Can everyone understand the problem statement?

If you have written a simple and short problem statement, then the probability is high that everyone on your team will understand it.

Alternatively, a brilliantly complex and arcane problem statement will not be as effective across the spectrum of your team! KISS!

I propose a simple test: Take your problem statement to a very junior member of your team and ask *that person* to explain what the problem statement means to *them*.

Probing Question #1-B: Is the problem statement compelling?

Is the wording of the problem statement going to engender heroics or yawns?

You will likely be asking much of your team – more work, more focus, more intellectual demands. Have you motivated them to deliver?

Words matter, and if the problem statement does not energize team members and compel action, you will likely be stuck in the doldrums.[12]

Spend the effort upfront to wordsmith a problem statement that creates energy!

> **Wordsmith a problem statement that creates energy!**

Consider the difference between "Build a booster with 7.5 million pounds of thrust" and "Create the lift vehicle to achieve Earth orbit to put a man on the moon in this decade." The first is a technical specification, and the second is a motivator. Go with the motivator every time.

Probing Question #1-C: Have all the customers and stakeholders concurred?

Once you have received inputs from all the customers and stakeholders (see chapter 7), then you must blend everyone's input into an easily understood problem that you will solve.

You may not be able to achieve 100 percent concurrence on the problem statement, so there will likely be trade-offs. That's life! Take the time to discuss the trade-offs with your stakeholders.

Probing Question #1-D: Has success been defined?

Integral to any problem statement is a definition of success.

Success has to be measurable.

Everyone on the team, from most junior to most senior, must understand

> **Success has to be measurable.**

---

12 The Doldrums refers to the ocean near the equator, where the wind is usually very light or nonexistent. In the days of sail, this meant little or no progress.

success. When describing success, great managers strike a balance between specificity and brevity. Too much specificity, and the goal loses people's attention. Too brief, and the outcome is too vague.

Consider the problem statement for the Apollo program Saturn V rocket team listed earlier: "Create the lift vehicle to achieve Earth orbit to put a man on the moon in this decade." Strategic – check. Specific and measurable – check. Speaks to everyone on the team – check.

From the strategic definition of success, each team can and should build their own problem statement with an attendant, more narrow definition of success.

Einstein and problem definition

Einstein is purported to have answered the question, "If you have one hour to save the world, how would you spend that hour?" by replying, "I would spend fifty-five minutes defining the problem and then five minutes solving it."

Spend the fifty-five minutes!

CHAPTER SUMMARY

- The task or project must solve a clearly stated and easily understood problem.
- The problem statement must be simple and short.
- Take a deep breath if you find yourself getting impatient; spend the time upfront to decide on and articulate what problem you are trying to solve.
- Take your problem statement to a junior member of your team and ask them to explain what the problem statement means to them.
- If everyone on the team knows the problem you are trying to solve, you are much more likely to be successful.
- Spend the energy upfront to wordsmith a problem statement that creates energy!
- The problem statement should define success.
    - ✓ Success has to be measurable.
    - ✓ Everyone must understand success.
    - ✓ The definition of success must strike a balance between specificity and brevity.

The Questions

Socratic Management Question:
- ✓ What is the problem we are trying to solve?

Probing Questions:
- ✓ Can everyone understand the problem statement?
- ✓ Is the problem statement compelling?
- ✓ Is the problem statement simple?
- ✓ Have all the stakeholders concurred?
- ✓ Have all the customers concurred?
- ✓ Has success been defined?

Articulate Why Solving the Problem Matters

Socratic Question #2: Why are we solving this problem?

The days of simplistic "Do it because I said so" are long gone. You need to make a strong case for solving this problem to your team and, just as importantly, to yourself.

In Simon Sinek's book, *Start with Why*, he makes the case for *first* understanding the *why*. Before anything else. Before *how* and before *what*.

But it's not just *understanding* the why – it's *articulating*, simply and concisely, the reason(s) why you are solving this problem.

Probing Question #2-A: Why is solving this problem important?

Everyone has priorities. And, unlike Dilbert's horrid boss, all your tasks/problems/issues cannot be Priority 1.

If this problem is low priority or unimportant, why is this problem worthy of your attention?

> Here's the problem, and here's why it matters.

Your job as a manager is to connect the proverbial dots for your team: Here's the problem, and here's why it matters.

Probing Question #2-B: How is solving this problem connected to the fundamental goals of the organization?

Every effective organization has a vision and strategic goals.

> If you cannot make the case that solving the problem is important *and* connected to the vision and strategy, then it's a distraction.

Every manager should be able to articulate how solving this problem is connected to said vision and strategies.

If you cannot make the case that solving the problem is important *and* connected to the vision and strategy, then this problem is a distraction.

Probing Question #2-C: What's in it for me?

Not every problem requires your management attention. There is (or will be) a plethora of problems clamoring for your time and energy. Why this one?

The acronym WIFM (What's in it for me?) [13] has been turned into a neologism, as in "What's the WIFM?"

In addition to identifying the importance of the problem and its connectivity to the vision/strategies, managing the solution to this problem should have personal importance.

In some cases, the answer is relatively simple: I want to please my boss. In other cases, it may be because you have a passion for this problem. What matters is that you understand your own WIFM!

Probing Question #2-D: Who *really* cares about solving this problem?

Another way to state "who really cares" is to ask "who is passionate" about solving this problem?

---

13   Theoretically, it should be WIIFM, but it has evolved to just WIFM.

As part of defining the problem, you should meet with major customers and stakeholders, internal and external, and question them about solving this problem.

One or more of your customers or stakeholders may be passionate about solving this problem. Know which one(s)! However, if none of your customers or stakeholders really care, perhaps you should revisit solving this problem.

Likewise, one or more of your bosses may be zealous about solving the problem. Know which one(s)! And if none of your bosses are passionately interested in solving this problem, that would sound a cautionary note.

Find out who on your team is a zealot on this issue. If no one on your team is fervent about solving this problem, then you have some serious motivational work to do!

Probing Question #2-E: What is the return on investment (ROI) for solving this problem?

A problem may be important, and people (some combination of stakeholders, customers, bosses, and team members) may truly care.

While you may not know precisely the investment necessary to solve the problem, you probably have a pretty good idea of the order of magnitude. In chapter 4, we cover the managerial importance of approximation and estimation. The evaluation of ROI is a great first place to estimate and approximate.

If the problem looks (at first glance) to have high cost and low return, then you should, at a minimum, go back to customers and stakeholders and educate them on your initial assessment of a low ROI.

CHAPTER SUMMARY

- Make a case for solving this problem to your team and, just as importantly, to yourself.
- Connect the dots for your team: Here's the problem and here's why it matters.
- If the case cannot be easily made that solving the problem is important and connected to the vision and strategy, then this problem is a distraction.
- Managing the solution to this problem should have personal importance.
- If none of your customers or stakeholders really care, perhaps you should revisit.
- If none of your bosses are really interested in solving this problem, that would sound a cautionary note.
- If no one on your team is fervent about solving this problem, then you have some serious motivational work to do!
- If the problem looks (at first glance) to have high cost and low return, then you should, at a minimum, go back to customers or stakeholders and educate them on your initial assessment of a low ROI.

The Questions

Socratic Management Question:

✓ Why are we solving this problem?

Probing Questions:

✓ Why is solving this problem important?
✓ How is solving this problem connected to the fundamental goals of the organization?
✓ Who *really* cares about solving this problem?
✓ What's in it for me?
✓ What is the return on investment (ROI) for solving this problem?

Identify the Customers and Stakeholders

7

Socratic Question #3: For whom are we solving this problem?

Earlier, I asked *why* are we solving this problem.

It's just as critical to know *for whom* we are solving the problem. For most nontrivial problems, there are customer(s), usually not singular, and stakeholders.

First, you need to identify them. Then you have to find out what problem they want solved.

Probing Question #3-A: Who are the customers?

First, what's a customer? While there are many definitions, a customer is considered an individual or organization that receives or purchases a product or service.

Now, who are your customers?

Probing Question #3-B: Are there multiple voices from a "single" customer?

It's easy to fall into the trap of considering the customer monolithic. But you can have multiple customers, and you can have multiple voices from one customer.

For complex problems, there is usually not a single customer.

To make things even more challenging, there are usually multiple voices from a single customer.

You can have multiple customers, and you can have multiple voices from one customer.

While you may get one payment, multiple constituencies within that customer may have contributed to that payment.

A nuclear submarine requires maintenance – some of it as simple as (literally) changing the oil, some of it extraordinarily complex. When I was Engineer Officer of *Pogy*, we traveled to Bangor, Washington, so that that the shipyard could perform an infrequent yet highly complex maintenance on the nuclear power plant. A good analogy would be replacing the cylinder rings on a car at 120,000 miles – you have to put the car on the lift, move a number of pipes and hoses out of the way, pull off the cylinder heads, pull out the pistons, replace the rings, and put everything back together again. And then test it. Yikes!

But that was not all. In addition to the shipyard, we had another maintenance facility doing many less-complex nonnuclear tasks (think replacing the windshield, trading out the muffler, and fixing a dent) as well as ship's crew doing routine stuff (think changing the oil).

My problem statement was deceptively simple: "Safely get all the work done correctly and get underway from Bangor on time." But I, as Engineer, had three customers – the shipyard, the maintenance facility, and ship's crew. Everyone was working for and getting paid by the Navy, yet each constituency/customer had different and often conflicting needs. It was a fun three months, and the only cast-iron rule I had was to run three miles during lunch each day to clear my head!

And we did finish on time. Safely.

Probing question #3-C: Who are the stakeholders?

First, what's a stakeholder? A stakeholder is an individual or organization affected by, or participating in, solving the problem.

Now, what people or organizations have a stake in the solution to the problem?

It's easy to answer this question poorly.

Think hard and look carefully; in almost every nontrivial real-world

There are likely many stakeholders beyond the obvious.

scenario, there are likely to be many stakeholders beyond the obvious.

Late in my Navy career, I became the second in command (think Chief Operating Officer equivalent) for a very large ship, a floating submarine repair facility. Like all ships, *McKee* (AS-41) required routine maintenance, albeit not as frequently because we had fewer sea miles on the odometer. Nonetheless, in the middle of my time onboard, we were scheduled for a four-month high-intensity period in dry dock.

As we were thinking about the problem we were going to have to solve, we realized that there were many stakeholders. Our crew – we needed to be safe. Our bosses – we needed to get done on time so *McKee* could get back to our primary mission. The nation – we needed to ensure a very expensive asset was maintained for the long run. Our contractor – we needed to support their workers so that their team could get the work done. The Navy base – we needed to get out of their dry dock on time. And there were many more.

But everyone had a stake in solving the problem. And we needed to work with and cooperate with all the stakeholders. In fact, in a few cases, we served as the referee between competing stakeholders.

Probing question #3-D: Have all the stakeholders opined?

In most (if not all) complex tasks, you, the manager, do not have the luxury of simply dictating the problem to be solved.

First, you have to know the customers and stakeholders. Then, you have to get their opinions and desires.

In our preparations for that four-month maintenance period, we spent lots of meeting time getting to know our partners and stakeholders, listening to their concerns and issues, and then formulating our problem statement (and the resulting plans) with them in mind.

Probing Question #3-E: Are they customers or are they really stakeholders?

Not all stakeholders are created equal; different stakeholders have different levels of involvement or importance.

Your list of stakeholders will be much longer than your list of customers.

It's easy to conflate customers and stakeholders.

It's easy to conflate customers and stakeholders. Sorting out whether someone or something qualifies as

| Follow the money.

a customer or a stakeholder matters because while you have to work with stakeholders, the customers are the ones who must be ultimately satisfied.

Probing Question #3-F: Have you followed the money?

"Follow the money" is not so much a question but an assertion.

If you have a very clear understanding of where the money comes from, it will cut through the fog and quickly clarify the customer relationship(s).

Get together with your contracting and financial team and understand who is paying for what, and how the money is coming to you.

CHAPTER SUMMARY

- Know for whom you are solving the problem.
- The customer is an individual or organization that receives or purchases a product or service.
- You can have multiple customers and you can have multiple voices within one customer.
- A stakeholder is an individual or organization affected by, or participating in, solving the problem.
- There are likely to be many stakeholders beyond the obvious.
- Follow the money to clarify the customer and stakeholder relationship(s).

The Questions

Socratic Management Question:

✓ For whom are we solving this problem?

Probing Questions:

✓ Who are the customers?

✓ Are there multiple voices from a "single" customer?

✓ Who are the stakeholders?

✓ Have all the stakeholders opined?

✓ Are they customers, or are they stakeholders?

✓ Have you followed the money?

SECTION 3

THE SIX QUESTIONS THAT CREATE A SOLUTION TO THE PROBLEM

In section 2, I asked three questions designed to clearly articulate the problem we are trying to solve. These Socratic questions helped to *define the problem*.

At this point, the reader should have created a clear problem statement that includes the underlying reasons for solving the problem and identifies customers and stakeholders.

In the following six chapters, we are going to use the Socratic method to help *solve the problem*.

Lay Out How to Solve This Problem

8

Socratic Question #4: *How* **are we going to solve this problem?**
How to solve this problem? List the overarching approach to be
taken. Focus on strategic (big picture), not tactical (detailed)
methodologies. Of course. Duh ...

Next chapter, please.

Not so fast, for behind that simple question lurk many nuances and complexities.

Ship repair, and nuclear submarine maintenance in particular,
are incredibly complex. Before every major maintenance period,
we would draw on a single (albeit very large) piece of paper our
overarching methodology. We resisted the urge to get into details – that would come later. We wanted to know and understand
the big picture.

For example, we usually had to do periodic inspections on
our electrical switchgear. That work involved turning off almost
every system on the ship. Sequencing that major disruption had
to be thoughtfully planned.

Sorting out the *how* is a great place to have all the stakeholders and customers involved in a group brainstorm.

For example, when we gathered in front of that big sheet of paper to lay out the upkeep, we invited the repair facility, the squadron (our bosses), and the shipyard representative to all provide input and concurrence on the big picture.

And of course, the larger the project, the bigger the piece of (virtual) paper.

Your focus is on the Socratic Management Paradigm – asking lots of questions using your experience plus your knowledge to help your team crystalize the answer to the top-level question "How will we solve this problem?"

Probing Question #4-A: Has this problem been solved before?
Don't reinvent the wheel. If someone else has previously solved this problem, then you likely have a gold mine of potential actions and (hopefully) lessons learned.

Even if the precise problem is slightly different, many methodologies can be drawn from analogous or similar problems.

This is where your experience and tapping into your network will help.

Probing Question #4-B: What do history and best practices tell us?

If the problem has been previously solved, then find out everything you can about history and best practices. Cast the net far and wide.

> **Find out everything you can about history and best practices.**

Certainly, don't make the same mistakes. Conversely, capture every shortcut and tip.

Probing history and best practices is where the manager needs to be very insistent on a thorough review of historical records.

Probing Question #4-C: How granular do you want to be?
A manager chooses how deeply to dig on the answer to the

question "How to solve the problem?" In some cases, the manager needs to know everything. In other cases, the manager needs only the top level of methodology.

There are many nuances that drive granularity. As a manager, make sure you make the level of granularity a conscious decision.

> **Make the level of granularity a conscious decision.**

Probing Question #4-D: What parts/tools/personnel do you need?

A great manager must probe deeply on the logistics – parts, tools, and personnel. While actions are important, if you do not

> **A great manager must probe deeply on the logistics.**

have parts/tools/people, you will not be successful. There are so many little ways to fail. This particular line of questioning is designed so that once you decide what to do, you have what is needed to do it.

> *For want of a nail the shoe was lost;*
> *For want of a shoe the horse was lost;*
> *For want of a horse the battle was lost;*
> *For the failure of battle the kingdom was lost—*
> *All for the want of a horseshoe nail.[14]*

Make sure you have a bag of nails!

Probing Question #4-E: What are you personally going to do?

The manager needs to decide early on what their level of "doing" and "managing" will be. Some people are micromanagers. And some are macromanagers.

First, match your level of involvement with the need. Second, make sure your level of involvement is a conscious choice, not a knee-jerk reaction.

---

14   A proverb that has come down in many variations throughout the centuries.

During my first six months as the newly minted CEO of the San Diego County Medical Society (SDCMS), I had zero confidence in our ability to track and manage money.

It started with a simple question to my then financial manager. I asked her to bring me the financials, which resulted in a stack of paper three-quarters of an inch thick. Complete, and totally useless except to another financial professional – which I was not.

Match your level of involvement with the need. Make your level of involvement a conscious choice.

Next, I asked her to give me a simple overview that told me, as CEO, how we were doing. Nope, couldn't do it. Needless to say, I became a micromanager of the financials – because I had to.

Two years later, when my new CFO had his feet solidly on the ground, I completely shifted my management style on financial matters! If it was a big number, I cared. Anything else, I knew he had a handle on it and that he would call me if it was important.

Probing Question #4-F: What are the interdependencies?

Except for the simplest of problems, almost everything is connected to everything else. Interdependencies are everywhere.

Look hard and look deep for connections with externalities (items you cannot control) and look as hard for internal interdependencies (items you can control).

Back to my example of the upkeep. We could control when we turned off the electrical switchgear to inspect them. But that impacted the ability of the cooks to feed the crew – no power, no ovens... so we needed to cook off the ship and bring the food onboard. So far, not too hard.

But then we found out that for several days, we would have no shore electrical power at all. During that outage, we needed to run our diesel engine to supply power, but that required the very

Interdependencies are everywhere.

switchgear we were going to shut down for maintenance. Things can get very complicated very quickly!

Probing Question #4-G: Have we "Red Teamed" this solution?
In chapter 3, we looked at what would go wrong with the Socratic Management Paradigm.

In this chapter, we explicitly ask what could go wrong as we solve the problem.

First, what's a Red Team? It is a highly capable and select group from inside the organization who are asked to be fierce internal critics. The Red Team is given license to look critically at every aspect of the plan. While the experience of being "Red Teamed" may not be pleasant, paraphrasing General Norman Schwarzkopf, "It is better to sweat in peace than bleed in war."

A great internal review process, epitomized by the Red Team, will flush out problems before these flaws have a deleterious impact on the plan.

Probing Question #4-H: What "Black Swans" have we identified?
The theory of Black Swan events was developed by Nassim Nicholas Taleb.[15]

A Black Swan event describes an incredibly rare but catastrophic event that comes as a complete surprise. Post-catastrophe, the failure to anticipate a "Black Swan" is explained away as simple folly, rather than as a management failure – and therefore no lessons are learned, and therefore another "Black Swan" event is possible.

Except that there are really no true Black Swan events. There are many Black Swan events that should have been anticipated

> **A "Black Swan" is an incredibly rare but catastrophic event that comes as a complete surprise.**

---

15   The term "Black Swan" originates from the (Western) belief that all swans are white because these were the only ones accounted for. However, in 1697 the Dutch explorer Willem de Vlamingh discovered black swans in Australia.

and are therefore mischaracterized. And there is the role of plain old-fashioned lack of foresight.

The Fukushima Nuclear Generating Station on the east coast of Japan's main island, Honshu, was built with a seawall because the Japanese knew full well that earthquakes and the attendant tsunamis occur frequently. Japanese folklore was quite specific regarding how high the tsunamis had historically reached. The peasants knew how bad it could get, and sometimes had gone so far as to mark the cliffs to show the highest rise of water. The designers of the station, unfortunately, chose to ignore the folklore and built an economically reasonable seawall for a statistically average earthquake-triggered tsunami. Except the earthquake of March 2011 was the largest ever in Japan. And the seawalls were half the height that they needed to be.

No one "Red-Teamed" or asked about a "Black Swan" event, and the near-cataclysmic meltdown was a direct result of a seawall built too low and backup power systems built in the path of the tsunami.

How a manager deals with an unhappy Red Team result or an unwelcome Black Swan analysis is where moral courage comes into play (see chapter 21).

Another example from history is appropriate. In the run-up to the Battle of Midway in June 1942, the Japanese dutifully "Red Teamed" the upcoming campaign. In a stunning and unwelcome predictor of the future, the war-game results showed that an unexpected American aircraft carrier force could easily surprise the Japanese while they were occupied with bombarding Midway Island, leading to defeat. The Japanese admiral threw out this unwelcome result, ignored the ramifications, and re-gamed the campaign until the dice roll gave the desired result: an overwhelming Japanese victory.

Lack of moral courage to plan for and deal with a potentially unhappy and unwelcome result is the sign of a poor manager and ineffective leader. Six weeks later, *precisely* as the initial war game had predicted, three American carriers surprised the Japanese. The resulting catastrophic loss of four of Japan's six irreplaceable large-deck carriers shifted Japan from the offensive to the defensive and accelerated the country's eventual loss of the war.

Great managers listen and act on the *potential* for bad news before it becomes actual bad news.

Great managers also actively seek out potential or actual bad news. While setting the culture of the organization is a leadership function, outstanding managers insist that their team bring them actual bad news immediately, and bring them the potential for bad news as soon as possible.

Great managers listen and act on the potential for bad news before it becomes actual bad news.

Rather than punish the bearers of bad news, reward them for potentially saving your skin!

My Commanding Officer on *Nautilus*, Dick Riddell, gave me a fabulous piece of advice when he signed my qualification card as a submerged Officer of Deck, the apex of a junior officer's first three years.

"If in doubt," he said, "call me. If in doubt about being in doubt, call me."

If in doubt call. If in doubt about being in doubt, call.

The gravest mistake you could make in Captain Riddell's world was not involving him early in the problem. And every direct report to me since then has received that same sage advice.

Probing Question #4-I: Have we done a pre-mortem?

In chapter 3, I suggested a pre-mortem to identify what could go wrong and how to prevent things from going wrong before they went wrong.

Before approving a project, I strongly recommend every manager convene a formal pre-mortem to go over the results of the Red Team, to review the findings of the team thinking about Black

Swans, and to get the principals and workers to highlight anything that could possibly go wrong based on history and best practices. Once the points of failure are identified, then the great managers act to minimize the impact of *all* the potential problems.

Probing Question #4-J: What's the definition of success?
Critical to every plan is a clearly articulated definition of success.

If you have no goal, no end point, no definition of victory, you will never get there. So make sure that your plan spells out the moment when the problem you so clearly stated will have been clearly solved.

Sometimes it's obvious – the goal is absolute. When I was responsible for a one-month maintenance period, success was defined by the ship back at sea with everything that we touched working correctly. Easy to say, hard to do.

Sometimes it's not nearly so obvious – the goal is relative. When I was responsible for the Medical Society, the metaphorical goalposts were a lot harder to see. In fact, we moved the goalposts every year. We were continuously improving, and the only goal we could see was to do better this year than last.

Sometimes the goal is subjective and therefore ephemeral. When I teach a leadership and management class, I want the participants to become better leaders and managers, but that's nearly impossible to measure. However, I suggest to them that success is defined by their ability to discuss, in subjective terms, where they want to be as leaders and managers at some point in the future.

It's not always easy to articulate success – but you have to try.

Once success is defined, promulgate the heck out of it.

Lord Mountbatten, the last British Viceroy of India, was given a clear mandate by the Parliament: get Britain out of the Indian subcontinent. He established a clear goal, which was to haul down the British flag in New Delhi on August 15, 1947. In his office, Mountbatten posted a very large piece of paper that showed, for that date, the number of days left to the goal. He had himself frequently photographed with the so-called Mountbatten calendar in the background. Everyone on all sides knew the goal,

It's not always easy to articulate success – but you have to try.

and acted accordingly. And for better or for worse[16] , the Union Jack did come down on August 15, 1947.

Probing Question #4-K: Do we need to change the definition of success?

Sometimes reality interferes with the best-laid plans. Leadership and management often intersect at this point. Great managers have to do their utmost to meet the stated goals, but when it becomes impossible to meet the goal,

A great manager – and their leader(s) – must have the moral courage to change the definition of success if the real world tells you that the goal is not achievable.

then the leader (or the manager if she is both leader and manager) has to have the courage to change the plan.

If you have clearly promulgated the goal, as did Mountbatten, then it is politically difficult to change it. You will lose face if you change the goal; you might even lose your job.

But if the goal is obviously unachievable, stamping your feet and yelling at the top of your lungs will likely not change the outcome.

A great manager – and their leader(s) – must have the moral courage to change the definition of success if the real world tells you that the goal is not achievable.

Easy to say, devilishly difficult to do.

So have the guts to accept the inevitable and change the goal to reflect the real world.

---

16   There has been much debate about whether the British exit was too rapid and left too many unresolved problems (ticking time bombs) on the subcontinent.

CHAPTER SUMMARY

- Ask lots of questions using your experience or knowledge to help your team crystalize the answer to the question "How will we solve this problem?"
- Don't reinvent the wheel.
- Find out everything you can about history and best practices.
- List the overarching approach to be taken.
- Make the level of granularity a conscious decision.
- Enable success by identifying parts, tools, and people.
- Match your personal level of involvement with the need.
- Make sure your level of involvement is a conscious choice.
- Most everything is connected to everything else.
- Ask what could go wrong.
- Set up a Red Team process.
- Look for Black Swans.
- Do a pre-mortem.
- Have a clearly articulated definition of success.
- Be ready to change the definition of success.
- Demand that your team comes to you with the bad news and the potential for bad news.

Questions

Socratic Management Question:

    ✓ *How* are we going to solve this problem?

Probing Questions:

    ✓ Has this problem been solved before?

    ✓ What do history and best practices tell us?

    ✓ How granular do you want to be?

    ✓ What are you personally going to do?

    ✓ What parts/tools/personnel do you need?

    ✓ What are the interdependencies?

    ✓ Have we "Red Teamed" this solution?

    ✓ What "Black Swans" have we identified?

    ✓ Have we done a pre-mortem?

    ✓ What's the definition of success?

    ✓ Do we need to change the definition of success?

Match People to Tasks

9

Socratic Question #5: *Who* will do what?

Once the question "How are we going to solve this problem?" has been answered, then the next question is "Who is assigned to do what?"

Probing Question #5-A: Is one person assigned responsibility for each task?

All of us have seen the disasters created by either the division of responsibility ("No, you're in charge..." "No, YOU are in charge.") or the abdication of responsibility (where no one is in charge).

A timeless principle of both leadership and management is that responsibility for any given task or role rests with a unique person. One. Not two or three. Not a committee. One person.

> **Responsibility for any given task or role rests with a unique person**

For each task, find out who is responsible. If no one is responsible, assign someone. If multiple people or a committee is responsible, assign one person as responsible. But this absolutely and emphatically does not mean that only one person is doing or working on the task. Only that one person is responsible.

Probing Question #5-B: Is the task matched to the person?

People are different. Tasks are different. It seems obvious, but many managers, particularly less experienced ones, allow people assignments to simply happen. Whoever drew the short straw gets the tough assignment.

The wise people at the Bureau of Naval Personnel understood that crewing the oldest and most challenging submarine in the fleet, *Nautilus*, was not for the average officer – hence only the top graduates got the "privilege" of serving on *Nautilus*. They matched task to person.

A great manager asks Socratic questions about personnel assignments and steers the right person to the right task.

Some people make great choices instinctively. The rest of us have to think about it.

First, we have to understand the needs of the task, as we explored in chapter 8. Then we have to think about our teammates. There are as many categorizations of talent as there are people. But you have to start somewhere.

Skills, knowledge, and talent

Martin Buckingham and his co-authors in the seminal book *First, Break All the Rules* assess three things that everyone possesses: skills, knowledge, and talent.

Skills are what you know how to do.

Knowledge is what you know.

Skills and knowledge can be acquired and are usually lumped together as experience.

Talent is what you have the capability of doing at some point in the future. Talent is innate and cannot be acquired.

> **Talent is what you have the capability of doing at some point in the future. Talent is innate and cannot be learned.**

Say you have identified a need for a new Chief Financial Officer (CFO) for a small-to-medium organization. The successful candidate should have a working knowledge of your accounting system and should be skilled at CFO-level tasks.

But that's not what I would use to filter for my next CFO. I want to know that the successful candidate would be creative and inventive and visionary – things you can't teach or impart. While skills and knowledge are prerequisites, they are not the final determinants – talent is!

Repair vs. produce vs. invent vs. vision

If you have to line up tasks and people, then you should probably think about categorizing tasks. I divide tasks into four broad categories, whether the object of the task is tangible or intangible: repairing, producing, inventing, or visioning.

> **Divide tasks into four broad categories: repairing, producing, inventing, or visioning**

If something is not working, whether tangible or intangible, the task is repair.

If something, whether tangible or intangible, does not presently exist in your circumstances – but someone knows how to create it – then the task is production.

If something does not exist anywhere, but you know you need it, then the principal task is invention.

If you don't know what you need, then the task is visioning.

Let's consider a real-world example. When I looked around as the brand-new CEO of the San Diego County Medical Society (SDCMS), I knew we were in trouble. Our finances and database were in bad shape, our membership trends were in worse shape, and the physical plant was in abysmal shape.

The problem I had to solve was to restore SDCMS to long-term health.

Task #1 – fix the database. If you don't know for sure who your members are, it's tough to communicate with them, and even harder to collect dues. I needed someone with great administrative skills to repair something that was broken. So, my most administratively savvy person got that task.

Task #2 – set up a new financial reporting system that would accurately provide me with actionable information about our money. This did not require invention (there were lots of systems out there), nor did it require repair (because we had nothing). I needed someone who could, using existing systems, produce something that worked for us. In the short term we outsourced it, and in the long term we brought on a CFO.

Task #3 – solve our lack of a proactive recruiting and retention process. Said a little differently, we had nothing to prevent people from leaving, and we had nothing to bring them in. Not a recipe for success! But interestingly, none of my peers had such a process, either. So we could not borrow or plagiarize – we needed to invent. I needed a creative person to invent a recruiting and retention process from whole cloth. Which we did.

Task #4 – we needed to envision a completely different medical society, one not dependent on a superseded business model (the solo practitioner in a dense urban environment) and aligned to the new practice modalities (the medium-to-large multispecialty group). I needed a visionary. This was the hardest task to align with a person. Ultimately, that person proved to be me, working hand-in-glove with the most enlightened of our elected leaders.

This last match of a task to a person highlights an interesting point. Sometimes, not often, you as the manager should perform, as opposed to manage, tasks. Be very circumspect about making this choice, because that can quickly lead to overload – but it is an option.

> **Sometimes, not often, the manager should perform, as opposed to manage, tasks.**

Plan vs. do vs. check

The "plan-do-check-act" cycle was created by W. Edwards Deming, considered by many the father of quality control. This iterative process is the foundation of both the scientific method and high-quality production.

Not surprisingly, the traits necessary to an effective doer are different from those required to plan and check.

Fixers, makers, inventors, and visionaries love doing things. But in broad strokes, you need more than doers. You also need planners and checkers.

> **You need more than doers. You also need planners and checkers.**

Some people have a knack for planning but are poor executors. Some are superlative in quality control and not so much in planning.

Task matching

Great managers know their people's strengths (and weaknesses) and match strengths to the tasks at hand.

Ask yourself whether a task is matched correctly to a fixer, a maker, an inventor, or a visionary.

Ask yourself whether the unique skills of planning and checking have been linked to those tasks.

Probing Question #5-C: Do people have enough bandwidth and/or priority to achieve assigned tasks?

Pathos is a quality that evokes pity or sadness. Dilbert, the comic strip that reflects the angst of the current American workplace, is replete with examples of characters who are assigned more work with less time to accomplish it. They have multiple Priority 1 work.

Your job as a great manager is to match people, bandwidth and/or priority, to tasks. That does not mean you shouldn't challenge people to do more – it means challenging your team to do more must be done intelligently, with careful examination and reexamination.

> **Match people, bandwidth and/or priority, to tasks.**

At the Medical Society, one of my team was incredibly talented and hard-working – and perpetually overloading himself.

He was always complaining about how hard he was working and how exhausting his job was, and that he needed to take some time off to recover. This was a death spiral in the making.

To combat this self-fulfilling prophecy, I asked him to write down all his tasks on a single sheet of paper, in priority order. We met weekly, and mutually decided on what tasks were realistically achievable *and* required, and their respective priorities.

I then gave him permission (and direction) to not take on those tasks on the back burner. Problem solved!

Probing Question #5-D: Have you matched passion to task?

You cannot buy, rent, borrow, or teach passion. It's organic. It can be stimulated, but it cannot be created. Just like talent.

> **If you are going to take on a difficult, challenging, and perhaps overwhelming task, you need a passion for the task.**

If you are going to take on a difficult, challenging, and perhaps overwhelming task, you need a passion for the task.

And on occasion, carefully channeled passion trumps almost everything else.

At the Medical Society, we were often asked to participate in volunteer events. One of my team had lost a close relative to a particularly nasty disease. When we were asked to provide support for an event from the nonprofit society addressing that illness, I did not even have to ask – she was already knocking at my door. Needless to say, the event was a great success because she was passionate about the underlying issue.

Probing Question #5-E: How's it going for you?

People are not machines. They need face-to-face attention and nurturing. It's not enough to simply assign a task and be done with it.

Periodically, sooner rather than later, great managers go out of their way to stay in touch and to communicate with their people. Many, many books have been written on this matter, so I will not attempt to reiterate them.

> **Great managers go out of their way to stay in touch and to communicate with their people.**

As part of the Socratic dialog between you and your team, you should be persistently and genuinely checking in with your team members.

Probing Question #5-F: How's it going for your team?

And you should not just enquire about your direct reports – your direct reports should likewise be stimulated by a Socratic question to check in with the members of their team.

Probing Question #5-G: What tasks are you outsourcing?

In today's distributed economy with so-called gig workers everywhere, you do not need to do everything within your organization. In fact, there are many arguments to be made for outsourcing many non-core tasks.

The Medical Society had published a monthly journal for more than 100 years. It never made money, production consumed great effort, and we were always challenged to find articles worthy of publishing.

Why, asked the new CEO, are we doing this all ourselves? The answer, of course, was not fulfilling. "Because we've always done it that way."

Needless to say we, in relatively short order, outsourced the production and advertising to the point we were no longer losing money. The core function, the acquisition of content, stayed under our control.

CHAPTER SUMMARY

- Responsibility for any given task or role rests with a unique person.
- People possess skills, knowledge, and talent.
- Skills and knowledge can be acquired.
- Talent is what you have the capability of doing at some point in the future.
- Talent is innate and cannot be acquired.
- Divide tasks into four broad categories, whether the object of the task is tangible or intangible: repair, production, invention, or visioning.
- Sometimes the manager may perform, as opposed to managing, tasks.
- You need more than doers. You need planners and checkers.
- Match people, bandwidth, and/or priority to tasks.
- You need passion for the task.
- Great managers go out of their way to stay in touch and to communicate with their people.
- Outsource most non-core tasks.

Questions

Socratic Management Question:

✓ *Who* will do what?

Probing Questions:

✓ Is one person assigned responsibility for each task?

✓ Is the task matched to the person?

✓ Do people have enough bandwidth and/or priority to achieve assigned tasks?

✓ Have you matched passion to task?

✓ How's it going for you?

✓ How's it going for your team?

✓ What tasks are you outsourcing?

Geography Matters

10

Socratic Question # 6: Where are we doing what?

Geography matters – even in this hyperconnected world where you can travel halfway around the globe on a longish day.

Not only geography but location. Where you do something, surprisingly, matters.

Many years ago, I was responsible for the material and maintenance for ten of the oldest submarines in the fleet. One day we discovered that the screw, the propeller, on one of our submarines needed replacement. The cause for this unfortunate requirement was a completely different and not-fun story.

The replacement screw for our San Diego–based submarine was on the other side of the country, in Norfolk, Virginia. And it was December. And we were in a hurry. And the screw dwarfed the normal tractor-trailer truck. And was seriously heavy. Now what?

Oh, and no cell phones or GPS.

We had to deal with distance, location, and weather all at once. Hopefully, you'll never have to spend Christmas micromanaging the movement of a really big object, but we got it to San Diego in time.

Geography mattered – and so did the weather.

Probing Question #6-A: Why are we doing that there?

While the answer may be totally reasonable, sometimes you will be amazed.

One of my least favorite answers to that question (or any question, for that matter) is "Because we've always done it that way."

Great managers listen carefully to the reasons for a location and sometimes suggest a new line of thinking about location.

After I'd been the CEO of the SDCMS for three years, we sold our termite-infested, poorly maintained, and high-overhead building. Where to now, everyone asked? Well, of course, two blocks down the street – we love that old location!

Not so fast, I said. Given that modes of practice have changed, the locus of our largest customers, the large and medium groups, may not necessarily be where we had the last building.

We got busy with maps, census numbers, and computer simulations. Eventually, we located about a mile from the old building, but it was a thoughtful decision, not a knee-jerk reaction.

Probing Question #6-B: How will weather affect our tasks?

If you are going to have a meeting in the Midwest in January, perhaps you should reconsider. If you are going to build a factory that requires lots and lots and lots of water, perhaps Southern California might not be optimal. If your industrial processes require exorbitant amounts of power (think Bitcoin mining), then you should go where the power is cheap and renewable because of hydroelectricity.

The number of possible impacts, particularly as the weather becomes more extreme, are endless.

One of my favorite sayings is "You can't change the weather, you can only dress for it – but do check the weather report!" And I'm speaking both literally and figuratively here.

> You can't change the weather, you can only dress for it – but do check the weather report.

Probing Question #6-C: How will the politics of a given location impact our tasks?

While we live and work in the *United* States, there are, regrettably, diverging geographic impacts on

> **Not everything needs to be done *in situ*.**

a variety of issues. A great manager is alert enough and sensitive enough to take shifting geographically related political winds into account.

Probing Question #6-D: What can be done virtually?

Not everything needs to be done *in situ*. Do you really need to bring ten people to a one-hour face-to-face meeting in Chicago in December? Perhaps not. But asking that kind of Socratic question is what being a great manager is all about.

CHAPTER SUMMARY

- Great managers listen carefully to the reasons for a location, and sometimes suggest a new line of thinking about location.
- You can't change the weather, only dress for it. But you have to check the weather report!
- Be alert to shifting geographically related political winds.
- Not everything needs to be done in person.

Questions

Socratic Management Question:
- ✓ Where will we do what?

Probing Questions:
- ✓ Where are we doing what?
- ✓ Why are we doing that there?
- ✓ How will weather affect our tasks?
- ✓ How will the politics of a given location impact our tasks?
- ✓ What can be done virtually?

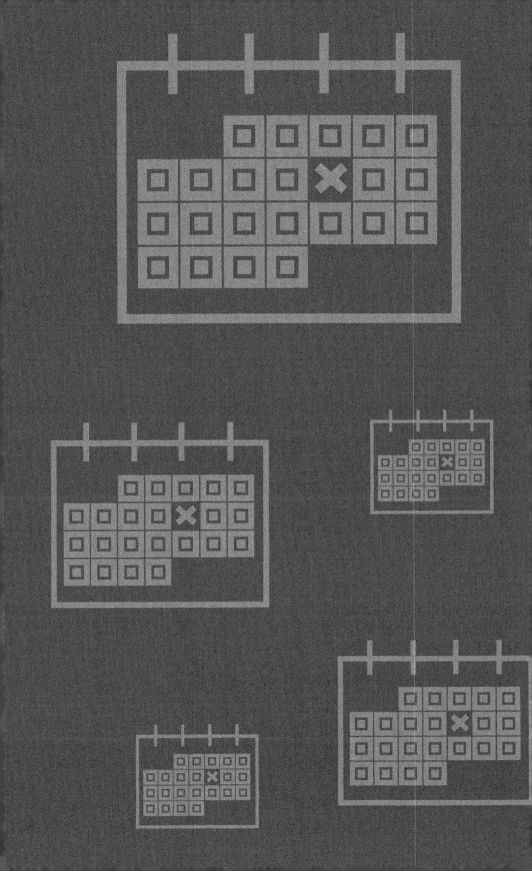

Check the Calendar

Socratic Question #7: When are we doing what?

This Socratic question is obvious. We live in a world that expects us to be on time. Great managers make schedules that tell everyone the timeline for developing and implementing the solution to the problem.

But fantasy schedules will not help you solve the problem.

Time and Priority

In most cases, "when" is a sign of priority. Sooner usually means more important. Later almost always spells low priority.

Probing Question #7-A: When are we doing the really hard stuff?

One of the Commanding Officers I dedicate this book to, Captain Wynn Harding, would always remind us that prime time was for prime tasks.

Let's say you are doing something hazardous that requires a lot of attention and would benefit from supervision. Specifically, you are going into 440-volt electrical panels to clean and test them.[17] You have two choices:

---

17 110 volts, what comes out of your wall socket, can kill you, while 440 volts can literally incinerate you.

✓ 1. Perform the hazardous procedure between midnight and 6 am, so as to not inconvenience the crew because you turned off the power to the galley (kitchen). This meant tired sailors would be working in switchboards with lethal voltages, and supervisors would have been up for a long time.

✓ 2. Perform the same hazardous procedure between 8 am and 4 pm with alert sailors and focused supervisors, and feed the crew cold sandwiches.

The crew proposed choice #1 – after all, who likes cold sandwiches? I chose #2 and obtained the concurrence of my captain – because he, like me, was trained by Admiral Rickover to do the right things and do them right at the right time. Sage advice.

So do the hard stuff when you and your people are fresh.

Probing Question #7-B: How much rest has your team had?

Caffeine only goes so far. Skipping time off is not that great of an idea. Going without sleep is not a badge of honor, but a testament to poor resource allocation and horrid planning.

Probe (and care about) how tired - emotionally, mentally, and physically - your teammates are.

And worry about your own stamina.

> **Do the hard stuff when you and your people are fresh.**

During both the Cold War and World War Two, the limiting factor in many submarine tactical situations was the lack of sleep of the Commanding Officer. On many submarines, the second in command (XO) politely shoved the Captain into bed during times with little or no projected action.

> **Man with two watches does not know what time it is.**

Probing Question #7-C : Can I see the master calendar?

It's been suggested that a man with two watches does not know what time it is. Likewise, an organization (even a family) without a master calendar can easily create schedule conflicts or schedule gaps.

Great managers insist that all the temporal events occupy one (figurative) piece of paper. And that (figurative) piece of paper should be prominently posted and frequently checked.

Current information technology makes maintaining a master calendar as well as sharing temporal information much easier, so take advantage of the tools.

Probing Question #7-D: What is going on outside the organization?

I was well along toward planning a visit to my son at college in the fall, when I had an epiphany – that's football season. I wonder if... and sure enough, the entire near-campus hotel room stock had already been reserved because of a home game. I should have checked the football schedule sooner!

In a similar collegiate vein, my son attended college on the East Coast and usually finished his fall term the day before Thanksgiving. I bought plane tickets in June because if I waited until October, the ticket prices would be exorbitant.

> Look hard at what else is going on outside your organization.

You have to look hard at what else is going on outside your organization.

Probing Question #7-E: What about environmental factors that are time related?

Perhaps you don't care about the tide, the moon, or the time of the sunrise/sunset.

Most of us are not are planning D-Day, where environmental factors became the driving force for setting the date. But if you're planning a convention in Miami in October, during peak hurricane season, or you need lots of daylight for a difficult equipment move, then you need to think about environmental factors.

Mother Nature can trip up your schedule just as easily as a scheduling conflict – and you can't argue with her!

Probing Question #7-F: What are the key events in the next major time frame?

While many of these probing questions are designed to be asked of others, this question is also helpful to you.

Many days when I was walking to the Medical Society break room, the SDCMS team would wonder if their CEO had lost his marbles, because I would walk, head down in concentration and mumbling to myself repeatedly, "OK, Tom, what are the critical events in the next three months? Three weeks? Three days?"

And as I answered my own questions, it allowed me to focus on the near term and make sure we had all the bases covered.

> **Mother Nature can trip up your schedule just as easily as a scheduling conflict.**

Many have explained situational awareness as one of the critical skills for leadership and management. I would posit that temporal awareness is just as important as situational awareness to getting things done!

> **Temporal awareness is just as important as situational awareness.**

Nothing focuses an organization like an upcoming deadline. But, unless you're a college senior, you can't wake up two days before a major deadline and decide to get to work.

Knowing what's on your time horizon is not optional!

CHAPTER SUMMARY

- Fantasy schedules will not help you solve the problem.
- In most cases, "when" is a sign of priority.
- Prime time is for prime tasks.
- Probe (and care about) how tired – emotionally, mentally, and physically – your team is.
- All temporal events should occupy one (figurative) piece of paper.
- Know the key events in your organization.
- Look hard at what else is going on outside your organization.
- Keep an eye on environmental factors.
- Knowing what's on your time horizon is not optional!

Questions

Socratic Management Question:

  ✓ When will we do what?

Probing Questions:

  ✓ When are we doing the really hard stuff?
  ✓ How much rest has your team had?
  ✓ Can I see the master calendar?
  ✓ What is going on outside the organization?
  ✓ What about environmental factors that are time related?
  ✓ What are the key events in the next major time frame?

Got Time?

Socratic Question #8: How long will it take?

Everyone who has ever taken on the marriage-defying task of a home remodel knows the Golden Rule: double the cost, double the time.

Great managers look extremely hard at two variables – time, which we will discuss in this chapter, and money, which we will discuss in the next chapter.

Your credibility and future effectiveness are directly linked to how accurately you can project and accomplish schedules, and deliver at or below budget.

Probing Question #8A: How do you know?

This Socratic question usually receives a heartfelt, strongly voiced, and optimistic answer.

Of course, we *know* that task xxx will take 5.37 weeks.

Right....

Great managers are healthy skeptics, a topic we will explore in greater detail in chapter 22. They want to know *how* your team came to this remarkably accurate conclusion that the task would take 5.37 weeks.

It doesn't take a lot of scratching to come up with hallucinogenic or miracle-dependent estimates.

Probing Question #8-B: What are the assumptions underlying this time estimate?

Every estimate, whether time or money, has underlying assumptions. Some are easily exposed. Some are deeply buried.

Great managers know that estimates are based on assumptions, and if estimates are to be believed and relied upon for other decisions, then these assumptions must be exposed, analyzed, and agreed to by all the relevant parties.

> **Estimates are based on assumptions, and these assumptions must be exposed, analyzed, and agreed to by all the relevant parties.**

Probing Question #8-C: What do history and best practices tell us?

Stockbrokers are fond of repeating the mantra their lawyers make them say over and over: "Past performance is no guarantee of future results."[18]

Great managers look to, and know, their history, as well the circumstances that created that history. So yes,

> **Look to past performance to project what the future might hold.**

look to past performance to project what the future might hold.

But don't stop with history. Ask "How long does it take the best, and why?"

If your past temporal performance lags the benchmarks, then that's another fertile field for Socratic inquiry.

Build some slack in the timeline

Experienced managers know that things come up. You cannot control everything. But you can build some slack into the timeline to allow for the unforeseen.

Always underpromise and over-deliver, on schedule as well as other key parameters.

> **Underpromise and overdeliver.**

---

18 Cynics would argue that past performance sure gives you a hint!

Probing Question #8-D: Can I see the timeline?

There are literally hundreds of tools that will take a rough schedule drawn on the back of a cocktail napkin and turn it into a smooth and professional-looking timeline. However, I recommend a healthy dose of skepticism about gorgeous charts and graphs; just because the presentation looks pretty does not make it accurate!

It is critically important to be able to look at the total schedule on a single (figurative) piece of paper, and then drill down as necessary into areas of potential concern.

Probing Question #8-E: What one tool are we using to track the timeline?

The tools don't matter – but your project can use only one tool to manage the schedule. Back to the idea about the man with two watches. You can drive your team and yourself crazy if you don't agree on one tool to track time.

Probing Question #8-F: What are the likely causes of schedule slip?

Perhaps Nostradamus[19] is out this week, so it might be difficult to project where schedule slip will occur. Note that I did not say "might," I said "will." Great managers probe very deeply and firmly into the possible causes for potential schedule slip.

And don't stop at the first and largest cause. Keep drilling down, as in the following example from my time as CEO of the Medical Society, where the execution of the Annual Ball was a critical event for the staff.

- o   Q – When will the invites for the Annual Ball be in the mail? A – Tuesday.
- o   Q – Are the invites stuffed in the envelopes? A – Well, no, they haven't come back from the printer yet.

---

19   A French astrologer, physician, and reputed seer best known for his book *Les Prophéties*, a collection of 942 poetic quatrains allegedly predicting future events.

- o Q – When will the invites come back from the print-er? A – Well, umm, we're not sure at this point.
- o Q – What is causing this uncertainty? A – Well, umm, the hotel has not yet provided the final ballroom lo-cation.
- o Q – And why is that? A – We can't seem to connect with the ballroom coordinator.
- o Q – Why is that? A – He's on vacation until Monday (one day before the invites are to be mailed).
- o Q – Would it help if I called the hotel manager? A – Oh yes, please!

Probing Question #8-G: What specific steps will you take to control schedule slip?

Once they've identified potential sources of schedule slip, great managers ask their teams to take specific steps to preclude those causes of schedule slip from materializing.

And as in the example above, sometimes the manager may be able to overcome barriers that the team might not be able to break down.

Probing Question #8-H: When is the next schedule review meeting?

Nobody likes meetings.

But gathering your team in an efficient and effective periodic schedule review meeting can identify problems and corrective action early enough to prevent schedule slip.

The two keywords are "efficient" and "effective." If the meet-ing drones on for hours until everyone is bored and frustrated, you won't get results. Likewise, if all the right players are not in the room, the underlings will likely be enthusiastic but not knowledgeable.

Great managers lead great schedule review meetings.

Probing Question #8-I: What happens if the schedule slips?

Dang. Despite your best efforts, your schedule is slipping. If you've asked the right probing questions early in the project, then you have a contingency plan in case of schedule slip. If you didn't ask the right probing questions, it's improv time. And you really don't want to do improv on big or small projects – it's entertaining, yes, but not likely to be successful.

> **Have a contingency plan in case of schedule slip.**

CHAPTER SUMMARY

- Look extremely hard at time and money.
- You want to know *how* your team came to the timeline.
- Know the assumptions your timeline is based on.
- Use history and best practices as benchmarks.
- Have a unified timeline.
- Have single timeline tool.
- Know the causes for potential schedule slips.
- Take action to preclude potential schedule slips.
- Have periodic schedule review meetings.
- Have a plan for a schedule slip.

Questions

Socratic Management Question:

    ✓ How long will it take?

Follow-on Probing Questions:

    ✓ How do you know?

    ✓ What are the assumptions underlying this time estimate?

    ✓ What do history and best practices tell us?

    ✓ Can I see the timeline?

    ✓ What one tool are we using to track timeline?

    ✓ What are the likely causes of schedule slip?

    ✓ What specific steps will you take to control schedule slip?

    ✓ When is the next schedule review meeting?

    ✓ What happens if the schedule slips?

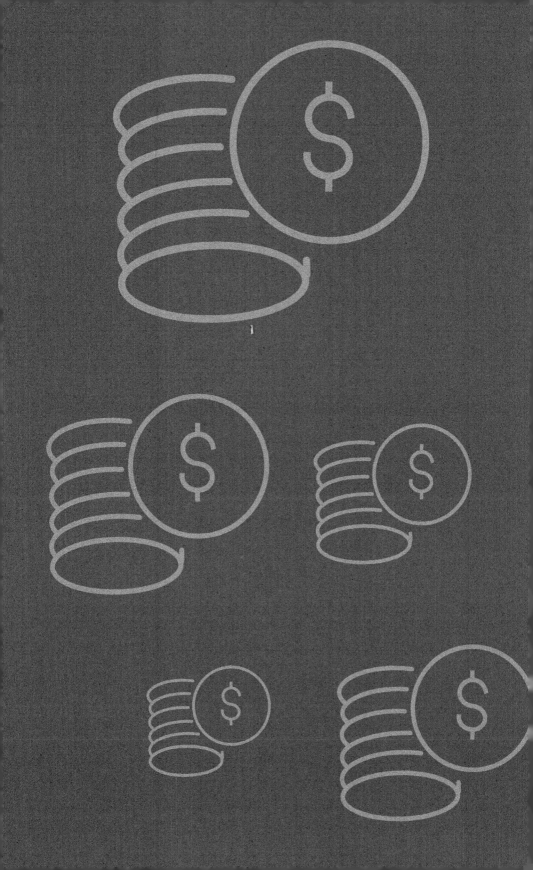

Got Money?

While time and money are clearly different and require different skill sets, the Socratic and probing questions are remarkably similar. In order to minimize repetition, I have eliminated explanations that are as applicable to time as they are to money.

Socratic Question #9: How much will it cost?
Knowing how much money it will cost is important, but remember that cost is not just about money. We are trained to equate cost and money. Great managers expand their concept of cost in many directions. Emotional cost. Opportunity cost. Nonfinancial resource cost. Climate cost. Political cost.

Probing Question #9-A: How do you know how much it will cost?

Probing Question #9-B: What are the underlying assumptions to the cost estimate?

Probing Question #9-C: What do history and best practices tell us?

Probing Question #9-D: Can I see the budget?

Probing Question #9-E: What one tool are we using to track the budget?

Probing Question #9-F: What are the likely causes of overbudget?
Causes of overbudget can be twofold: under revenue or over expenses.

Every year at our Medical Society gala, we managed for a revenue-neutral budget. But different honorees had different tastes. If we were going to serve a sumptuous meal, we needed to raise ticket prices. Not popular, but choices have consequences!

If, on the other hand, a simple buffet was acceptable to that year's honoree, we could drop the prices. It seems obvious, but great managers make cost trade-offs with their eyes wide open.

Probing Question #9-G: What specific steps will you take to control overbudget?

Probing Question #9-H: When is the next budget review meeting?

Probing Question #9-I: What happens if the budget goes into the red?

Probing Question #9-J: Where are the contingency budget lines?
Just as in creating believable timelines, the great manager builds enough slack into the budget to manage uncertainty.

Leave a not-insignificant budget line item for contingencies.

Golden rule of budgeting

Great managers are liberal (overestimate) on expenses and conservative (underestimate) on revenue. Let all your surprises be to the upside!

> **Overestimate expenses and underestimate revenue**

CHAPTER SUMMARY

- Look extremely hard at time and money.
- You want to know *how* your team came to the budget.
- Know the assumptions your budget is based on.
- Use history and best practices as benchmarks.
- Have a unified budget.
- Have a single budgeting tool.
- Know the causes for potential budget overruns.
- Take action to preclude potential budget overruns.
- Have periodic budget review meetings.
- Have a plan for budget overruns.

Questions

Socratic Management Question:

   ✓ How much will it cost?

Follow-on Probing Questions:

   ✓ How do you know how much it will cost?
   ✓ What are the underlying assumptions to the cost estimate?
   ✓ What do history and best practices tell us?
   ✓ Can I see the budget?
   ✓ What one tool are we using to track budget?
   ✓ What are the likely causes of overbudget?
   ✓ What specific steps will you take to control overbudget?
   ✓ When is the next budget review meeting?
   ✓ What happens if the budget goes into the red?
   ✓ Where are the contingency budget lines?

IMPLEMENTING
THE PLAN

Stating the problem and identifying a solution are not enough.

The final two Socratic questions are designed to help great managers *implement* the solution to the current problem, and *improve* on solving the next problem.

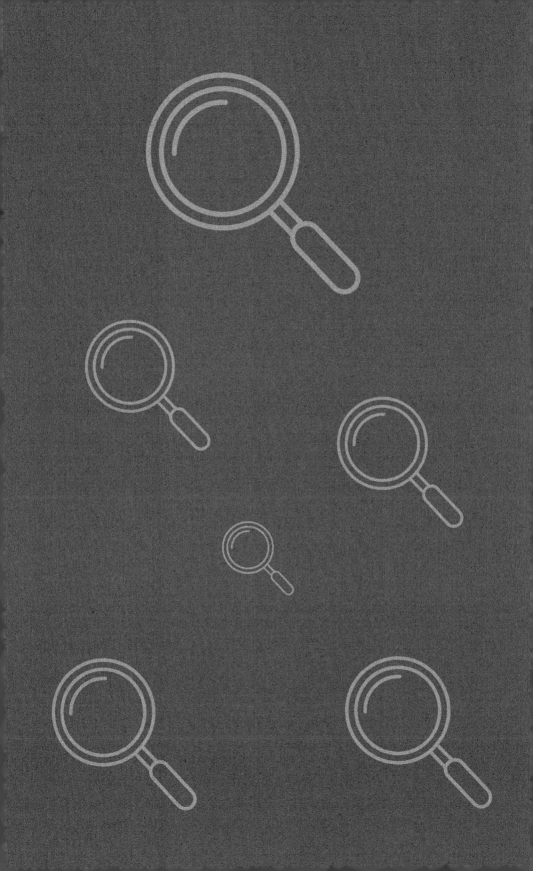

Monitoring

Socratic Question #10: How are we doing on the plan?

This Socratic question features two elements:

First, it assumes that there is an effective plan.

Second, it probes for progress on the work of the plan.

Probing Question #10-A: We do have a plan, right?

After all the questions and answers explored in Section 3, I assume that you have a plan. A plan you can see on a screen or on a piece of paper.

In earlier chapters, I discussed having a single timeline document and a single budget document. There's obviously more. Great managers have a great plan that connects people, actions, money, parts, and time.

If you don't have a unified plan, go no further until you have a *unified* plan in hand.

Discussing progress

I hate meetings. Most people can't stand them. But if you're managing a project, large or small, you need to periodically review status with your team.

Done poorly, reviewing status as caricatured in the comic strip Dilbert is unidirectional drivel. And hugely frustrating.

> **Great managers run great status meetings.**

Great managers run great status meetings as a vital bidirectional information transfer.

Probing Question #10-B: When is our next project status meeting?

There are many techniques to make this information transfer efficient. But what matters is not so much the technique you use, as the discipline of periodically exchanging information and ideas.

Probing Question #10-C: What system are we using to track progress?

There are literally thousands of project management systems – pick one and live with it. Use what works.

And don't succumb to the temptation to change to a "better" system in the middle of a project. The old adage about not changing horses in midstream comes to mind!

Once a project has kicked off, great managers must track progress. To track progress, you need a system that takes the status of the work and turns it into actionable information for both workers and managers. Great managers insist on the team-wide use of a reporting system.

The sophistication of project planning and monitoring software ranges from a large sheet of paper to multimillion-dollar systems that require a small army of IT specialists.

When I kick off a project, I use a large sheet of 11x17" paper (so old-fashioned and yet so effective for me).

When Boeing builds a new airplane, they use a super-computer.

The tool will scale to the project, but you cannot manage a project without a progress-tracking tool.

Probing Question #10-D: Is everyone *actually* using the designated system?

Having a single project system for planning and monitoring is one thing. Making sure everyone is using it is quite another.

Your system will have limits. They all do. Some of your team will have a "better" system and will pay lip service to the designated system. Pretty soon management will not be able to keep up because you are tracking status with multiple disconnected systems.

This is one of the very few spots where a manager needs to be dictatorial. Practice saying the following: "We will use this one project tracking tool, and everyone will be on it. Period."

A great follow-on question is "How do you *know* that everyone is using our designated system?"

Probing Question #10-E: Is the data being updated?

If the members of your team are not updating status promptly, the system will not provide accurate information.

Garbage In, Garbage Out – GIGO.

A great follow-on question is "What is the *frequency* with which we are updating the designated system?"

Probing Question #10-F: What's our goal?

Is there an end state? Is there a solution that defines victory? Is there a goal?

The problem statement developed in chapter 5 should have a strategic goal. But for anything except small projects, great managers know that there will be multiple incremental goals.

> **At any one time, there should be one clearly visible and understood goal.**

But at any one time, there should be one clearly visible and understood goal.

Probing Question # 10-G: Are we there yet?

Everyone has been on a long family outing, where at some point a youngster in the back seat chimes in with that oft-heard lament: "Are we there yet?"

Great managers know to ask and keep asking, "Have we met the criteria for success?"

> Have we met the criteria for success?

Not like the whiny eight-year-old in the back seat, but rather in the focused and thoughtful manner of someone working to keep the team on track.

And it is all about staying on track! It's about constantly asking how close to the *current* goal we are, knowing full well that there will likely be follow-on goals.

Probing Question #10-H: Have you gone and looked?

One of the most important management lessons I learned occurred on my first night underway on *Pogy*. My boss, Commander (later four-star Admiral) Archie Clemins, was deeply experienced. I was a brand-new Engineer Officer.

In the middle of the night, my engineering team asked to shut down a piece of equipment because of a leak that needed fixing. Being a dedicated soul, and not wanting to live with a material problem, I dutifully tromped up to the captain's stateroom and asked for permission to take that piece of equipment offline to repair it.

My captain opened an eye and asked me only one question: "Tom, have you gone and looked?"

Of course, I had not. And then I did. And my approach to repairing that fault was completely different once I looked at it with my own eyes.

And I learned a lifelong lesson: Never underestimate the power of looking at the problem yourself.

> Never underestimate the power of looking at the problem yourself.

There is a bonus to looking for yourself. If your team knows that you will look yourself, they will work harder to bring you better answers.

Probing Question #10-I: Have you positioned yourself where you can see clearly?
Great managers know when and where to position themselves for maximum impact.

If you are everywhere, you will quickly run out of usable hours in your day. If you are nowhere, then people will correctly assume that you don't care or don't know.

Finding the balance is the sign of a great manager.

Every time, or nearly every time, the ship pulls into port, you shut down the reactor and go on shore power. So, every time, or nearly every time, you get underway, you have to start up the reactor. Starting up a nuclear reactor on submarines is considered routine, and the engineering team is well-schooled in the process, which is explicitly documented and not hugely difficult.

Interestingly, this four-to-six-hour procedure almost always occurs in the middle of the night. So, if we wanted to get underway at 10 a.m., we would commence the reactor startup at roughly 2 a.m. – when people are pretty tired! And tired people sometimes do stupid stuff.

Our governing documents state that I could pick up the phone in my comfy bed at home and grant permission to start up without even being physically present.

I decided I'd be physically present in the plant for each and every startup. For almost four years. Not my wife's favorite thing, particularly because, as she quickly found out, it was not a requirement. But this was an evolution that I never wanted to get wrong. Ever.

I stayed out of the way during the relatively risk-free parts, but my eye was always on where things might go awry. And anyplace I could teach and impart experience, I would do so.

And the concept is not just applicable to things mechanical.

Every year at the Medical Society gala, several hundred doctors and VIPs gathered in a glittering venue. This shindig was a big deal to us. We needed to be perfect. So my COO, the gala organizer, and I were at the venue two or three hours before the first guest, just walking around, looking around, making sure that everything was on track – and ready to apply whatever attention was needed to an emergent problem. If we were bored, that was good. If we were running around with our hair on fire, that was bad, but the problem was solved before the guests arrived.

So great managers position themselves where they can teach and simultaneously prevent bad things from happening.

> **Great managers position themselves where they can teach and simultaneously prevent bad things from happening.**

Probing Question #10-J: Have you asked, "Why? Why? Why? Why? Why?" until you get to bedrock causality?

Bad things are going to happen. Mistakes will get made. Hopefully, you will catch the problems while they are small.

It's easy to treat little problems as anecdotal. But every little problem is a sign of a bigger problem to come. I will cause proofreaders everywhere to go nuts because I will repeat that for emphasis.

Every little problem is a sign of a bigger problem to come.

Great managers refuse to treat little problems as anything except a precursor to bigger problems. They probe and dig and ask until they come to the root cause of the (little) problem. Because until you have identified the root cause, you will not permanently prevent a recurrence of the little problem, or prevent the little problem from mushrooming into a huge problem.

> **Great managers refuse to treat little problems as anything except a precursor to bigger problems.**

Senior submariners have a focus on cleanliness and preservation that borders on OCD[20]. Most of the younger crew and the junior officers are perpetually annoyed that the senior officers insist that everything is meticulously painted and spotlessly clean. "Why," they ask, "does the propulsion plant need to be so darn clean? We're not running a #!*^@ hospital operating room here!"

One day during my end-of-watch tour on *Pogy*, I noticed a streak of rust on the gleaming white insulation on a seawater pipe. "Now that's odd, that wasn't there yesterday," I remarked to myself. At that point, I could have figuratively shrugged my shoulders, rationalized that rust will always exist in a seawater environment ("Hey, this is a ship at sea"), and kept on walking. Heck, it was pizza night, and I was hungry.

Having been well trained to investigate even the smallest discontinuity, I listened to the voice in my head and felt the insulation. It was soggy and wet, not bone-dry as it should have been. "Now that's odd, why would that be wet?" I remarked to myself.

We gathered a team, carefully removed the insulation, and found seawater where it should not have been. "Now that's odd, seawater shouldn't be there," we all remarked to ourselves.

Pretty soon we had a team furiously chasing down the root cause of the ever-so-slight amount of seawater running down the pipe. Way, way up in the overhead of the engine room, where no one could see it from the walkway, we found a seawater valve that was dripping from one of its fasteners. "Now that's odd, why would a seawater fastener exposed to Mother Nature's remorseless hand be dripping?" we all wondered to ourselves with furrowed brows.

After taking the appropriate precautions, we investigated and discovered something both interesting and scary: one of the bolts had not been properly fastened. "Now that's odd, why would that bolt not be properly torqued?" we asked ourselves with serious

---

20 Obsessive Compulsive Disorder. Learned that one from my wife the psychiatrist!

worry, because for all we knew, there might be many more loose bolts, any one of which could cause a flooding casualty.

And we were painfully aware that in our lifetimes, two American nuclear submarines had been lost with all hands due to flooding.

We could easily have retorqued the offending fastener, declared victory, and gone forward to grab some of that yummy pizza and watch the evening movie.

Nope.

"Why was this fastener not properly torqued?" I asked.

"And, which other fasteners do we need to check to make sure they were properly torqued?" came the follow-on question.

We found the root cause of the problem and corrected it, making sure that no other fasteners were improperly torqued.

That was a powerful reminder about why we kept everything meticulously painted and spotlessly clean: not to please the brass walking through the ship, but so we could easily spot the deviation from the norm.

And once we spotted a deviation from the norm, we kept investigating until we found the bedrock of causality. And then we fixed the problem. Permanently.

> **Once we spotted a deviation from the norm, we kept investigating until we found the bedrock of causality.**

So great managers know that every time you review financials or admin or anything else, assume there's a problem in there that's going to bite you if you don't find it – you're just not looking hard enough.

Another, perhaps pedestrian, example from home is appropriate – to make the point that asking "Why? Why? Why? Why? Why?" is not just the purview of submarines at sea.

Several months ago, my wife asked me to figure out why her delicates were getting torn every time they went in the wash.

That's odd – the washer-dryer system is not designed to create problems like torn silk or linen. Time for my trusty flashlight.

The washer didn't look unusual, but the drier lint screen had tiny bits of linen or silk residue on the screen top where it met the housing. Looking closer, the cover was not flush, and therefore the edge of the cover was sticking out and snagging the delicates. Aha, problem solved.

Wait, why is the lint screen not flush (smooth) with the housing? I pulled the screen and noticed that I could only get the screen flush by pushing down hard. That's odd. Why would the screen not go all the way down? My trusty flashlight just showed a dark bottom of the housing. Better get the super-duper flashlight.

And there, at the bottom of the lint screen housing, was a handful of lint compressed into a rock-hard mass. It was a fire hazard looking for a time to ignite.

The offending lint was soon gone, but the lesson is timeless.

Investigate every discontinuity. Ask "Why?" until you determine the root cause. And always listen to your wife when she reports a problem!

> **Investigate every discontinuity. Ask "Why?" until you determine the root cause.**

Probing Question #10-K: How will you correct this problem?
Great managers know that most people get up in the morning and want to do a great job. Most, but not all.

Some fraction, and I arbitrarily assign the percentage to be 3 percent, are misdemeanor dumb. They are not ill-intentioned, but they are just not capable. A smaller fraction, and I again arbitrarily assign the percentage to be 2 percent, are felony sociopaths. They just don't care, they willingly refuse to learn, and they often do bad things for bad reasons.

When you identify corrective action for a problem, you can follow one of two paths: create systems that assume that people want to do the right thing or create systems that assume people are either dumb or malignant.

Let's say that a work center supervisor exceeded her budgetary allowance. When you dig deep, you learn that it's quite difficult to find the most current balance and that it's not always up to date – and therefore easy to exceed the allowed balance, even when you don't mean to.

And this supervisor is a diligent and competent person, not stupid or malicious.

One approach is to require every expenditure to be approved by the accounting manager, who is then required to check the account balance. Simple, yet designed to frustrate everyone – the work center supervisor now must reach out to the accounting manager, who has to drop what he is doing to bring up the accounting system... So everyone is going to be annoyed and progress will slow down. The proposed solution treats people as though they are misdemeanor dumb or felony sociopaths. But, it's an "easy" fix for the manager.

Here's another approach. Fix the system so the account balance is easy to find and guaranteed to be up to date. Perhaps a bit harder in the short term but fixes the root cause of the problem and treats people as well-intentioned.

Probing Question #10-L: Can you "Improvise, Adapt, and Overcome"?

Assume that you have a plan that will solve the problem you articulated. Have you built in contingencies?

A universal truth is that no plan ever survives first contact with reality.[21]

Great managers probe to see what contingency plans

> **No plan ever survives first contact with reality.**

---

21 The original quotation was from German Field Marshal Helmuth von Moltke in the mid-nineteenth century.

have been created. In chapter 3, we talked about pre-mortems, Red Teams, and Black Swans.

But you still might not have thought of everything.

In the 1986 movie *Heartbreak Ridge*, the actor Clint Eastwood played a grizzled Marine gunnery sergeant leading a small, elite team. He growls repeatedly as only Clint Eastwood can, "Improvise, adapt, and overcome."

Great managers, perhaps not using those exact words, probe and mentor their teams so that they are resilient in the face of unexpected problems.

And when the totally unexpected and unplanned for happens, your attitude will carry you through.

In the middle of the Indian Ocean on *Pogy*, a really, really long way from anywhere, I received the unpleasant news that a very large pump, one of only two that moved water around the ship, was sounding like a dying washing machine and needed a new bearing. Shortly thereafter, it died. Dead. Frozen. Wouldn't turn with a crowbar.

We needed a new bearing.

OK, pull out a new bearing from supply – we have those, right? No problem. Oh wait...big problem. The replacement bearing was rusted through and through, because for whatever reason (we never did find out the cause) the part we had in stock was bad and the next parts warehouse was about 3,000 miles away. In another ocean.

Now what?

Improvise, adapt, and overcome.

One of my insanely creative mechanics, when given license and incentive to improvise, came

> **Improvise, adapt, and overcome.**

up with the brilliant idea of making our own bearing. Out of graphite[22]. We would improvise a mold, melt the graphite, pour it

---

22 Graphite is a common bearing material that allows a rotating element, the shaft, to rub with little or no friction against a stationary element, the bearing, thereby keeping the shaft steady.

into the mold, and presto – temporary bearing. Not perfect, not a long-term fix, but gets us to the next pit stop and a visit to the express line at the submarine parts warehouse.

OK, where's the graphite? Ummm, we don't ... Oh wait, we have a bajillion pencils and pencil lead is graphite! So for the next couple of days, the entire crew was scavenging pencils, shaving off the wood, melting the lead, and the next thing you know, the pump was running again.

Improvise, adapt, and overcome.

Oh, and we gave that mechanic a medal right on the spot. And ordered a whole lot more pencils. And a good bearing. And we made damned sure it wasn't rusted. And we checked all the other critical spare bearings to make sure they weren't rusted, either.

CHAPTER SUMMARY

- A great plan connects people, actions, money, parts, and time.
- Go no further until you have a plan in hand.
- Disciplined and periodic status meetings are a vital bidirectional information transfer.
- Have a system that takes the status of the work and turns it into actionable information for both workers and managers.
- Insist on the team-wide use of a reporting and progress management system.
- Status garbage in, status garbage out.
- There will be multiple incremental goals.
- At any one time, there should be one clearly visible and understood goal.
- Have clear criteria for success.
- Never underestimate the power of looking yourself.
- If your team knows that you will look yourself, they will work harder to bring you better answers.
- Position yourself where you can teach and simultaneously prevent bad things from happening.
- Every little problem is a sign of a bigger problem to come.
- Probe and dig and ask until you discover the root cause of the (little) problem.
- Maintain your systems so you can easily spot the deviation from the norm.
- Once you see a deviation from the norm, keep digging until you find the bedrock of causality. Then fix the problem permanently.
- Treat people as well-intentioned, not as felons or morons.
- No plan ever survives first contact with reality.
- Improvise, adapt, overcome.

Questions

Socratic Management Question:

- ✓ How are we doing on the plan?

Follow-on Probing Questions:

- ✓ We do have a plan, right?
- ✓ When is our next project status meeting?
- ✓ What system are we using to track progress?
- ✓ Is everyone actually using the designated system?
- ✓ Is the data being updated?
- ✓ What's our goal?
- ✓ Are we there yet?
- ✓ Have you gone and looked?
- ✓ Have you positioned yourself where you can see clearly?
- ✓ Have you asked, "Why? Why? Why? Why? Why?" until you get to bedrock causality?
- ✓ How will you correct this problem?
- ✓ Can you improvise, adapt, and overcome?

Learning

15

Inquisitiveness

This final Socratic question and the follow-on probing questions are all about curiosity.

The questions are about strategically analyzing the totality of the project, and answering the two most important "whys" – "Why did we fail?" and "Why did we succeed?" and then doing something productive with those answers.

Be a curious manager!

Socratic Question #11: How are we learning and improving?

The last Socratic question is deceptively simple – "How are we learning and improving?"

An oft-repeated and wise saying is "You're either getting better or you're getting worse."

One crucial difference between run-of-the-mill managers and great managers is the speed at which they learn and improve.

> **The difference between run-of-the-mill managers and great managers is the speed at which they learn and improve**

Probing Question #11-A: Is there a lesson learned in this failure?

At IBM, the company my father worked at for his entire career and where I was a summer intern, there circulated a famous anecdote about failure and learning.

A $10 million-dollar project had not gone well. Big money in those days. The then-boss of IBM, an irascible genius named Thomas J. Watson Sr., called the responsible manager to headquarters in Armonk, NY. When the shaken executive was asked by the supremely cranky Mr. Watson why he thought Mr. Watson wanted to see him, the executive replied that he expected to be fired for his failed project.

Mr. Watson is reported to have exploded, and paraphrasing, said, "Fire you? Why would I fire you when I just spent $10 million teaching you something? Now, what did you learn?"

As discussed in chapter 14, great managers ask why until they find the bedrock of causality.

Usually, there is short-term remedial action and long-term systemic corrective action.

Great managers are always looking for the root cause – and once identified, they spread the word on the underlying problems and solutions to everyone who needs to know.

Probing Question #11-B: How are we getting better?

It's not just failure that engenders learning. There are opportunities for improvement everywhere. Great managers are constantly asking themselves, and their teams, how something that is working well could be made to work better.

Millions of words have been written about continuous process improvement, but it all starts with the manager asking this simple Socratic question.

Probing Question #11-C: How do we promulgate lessons learned?
When something bad happens, tell everyone who needs to
know[23]. That takes courage. And courage is a managerial trait we
will explore in chapter 21.

Communicate in a way that is
not embarrassing, if you can, but
the price of avoiding the same
bad thing happening twice is
well paid.

> **When something bad happens, tell everyone who needs to know.**

And if your organizational culture hides mistakes, find some-
place else to work.

On my first long deployment to the Indian Ocean on *Haddo*,
a valve that controlled the operation for two of the four torpedo
tubes failed. Having a submarine with 50 percent of her weapons
suite non-operational was really not a good idea, but we did not
have the parts or tools to repair that valve, nor could we make the
repair parts onboard.

When we pulled into our next port, we worked overtime with
our Australian partners to repair the valve and put the torpedo
system back in operation. Normal wear and tear, no systemic
problems, success! Everything checked out and off we went.

Periodically, submarines fire practice torpedoes to make sure
that crew and ship are able to fight if called upon. No one wanted
a reprise of the disasters during the first year of World War Two
when nothing in the weapons suite worked.

After *Haddo* returned from deployment, we shot exercise torpedoes – and the first torpedo launched using the repaired valve
did not run properly. Must have been a bad torpedo. Load up the
next tube!

My inquisitive nature kicked in, and questioned the coinci-
dence – let's see, we fixed that valve six months ago and the first
real torpedo we shoot using that valve fails.... Hmmmmm.

---

23 The wise manager knows the difference between making a fool of themselves
in public and effectively communicating an important lesson learned.

At that point, we stopped everything. We brought the shipyard technical team onboard and quickly discovered that, while we had done everything by the book in Australia, there was an adjustment to these particular valves that only occurred during major shipyard maintenance – and the adjustment was not in the technical manual, which I had read and re-read. Therefore, no one outside the shipyard knew about it. Double secret probation, indeed.

Huge lessons learned. Quickly and easily fixed. And then we made sure that every submarine in the fleet knew that if they touched this valve, there was more than a simple operational test, thereby avoiding the "gotcha!" that befell us. And we updated the technical manual.

And it's not just negative lessons that are promulgated. If things are going well, share that also.

When I was CEO of the Medical Society, we published a monthly magazine. We went out of our way to find articles that would help physicians become more effective. Anytime someone did something really well that would help the rest of the community, we published it. [24]

When something good happens, tell everyone.

When something good happens, tell everyone.

Probing Question #11-D: How do we spread the intellectual wealth?

There were many reasons why the Japanese lost the Second World War in the Pacific. But the loss of carrier air superiority was certainly a major contributor.

From Pearl Harbor to the Battle of Midway six months later, Japanese naval aviation was unstoppable. They had the best planes, far and away the best pilots, and the results were mortally obvious.

---

24 The wise manager knows how to communicate success without bragging or boasting.

But the Japanese never rotated their combat-experienced pilots back home to train the next generation. Part of it was sheer numbers, and part of it was philosophy (i.e., "You're great, stay on the front lines!"). The Japanese Navy was eating their seed corn, in the language of the Midwest farmer.

The Americans, on the other hand, albeit with greater numbers, made a conscious decision to rotate the experienced pilots back to teach the next generation.

After eighteen months, the differences became very obvious. The Americans had invested in teaching the next generation, and the Japanese had not.

So even while you are in the middle of managing the current problem, think about how you will train your team and the next generation for the next problem. No fair hoarding talent!

CHAPTER SUMMARY

- Be a curious manager.
- The difference between average managers and great managers is the speed at which they learn and improve.
- What did you learn from this mistake?
- Constantly ask how something that is working well could be made to work better.
- When something bad happens, communicate it so that it doesn't happen again.
- When something good happens, communicate it so that it happens again.
- Think about how you will train your team and the next generation for the next problem.

Questions

Socratic Management Question:

✓ How are we learning and improving?

Follow-on Probing Questions:

✓ Is there a lesson learned here?

✓ How are we getting better?

✓ How do we promulgate lessons learned?

✓ How do we spread the intellectual wealth?

CASE STUDIES

Now that I've shown you the Socratic Management Paradigm and discussed the eleven questions great managers ask and answer, it's time to put the model to work.

In the following four chapters, I will present case studies, hypothetical but based on actual events, of managers using the Socratic Management Paradigm to address complex problems.

I will present a role, outline a scenario, and then challenge you, the reader, to think about how to manage the case study.

To obtain maximal learning benefit, I suggest you draft a problem statement, pick the key questions you would ask, and indicate what answers to those questions might not be acceptable.

I encourage the reader to think through the case study *before* turning the page to my thoughts.

To get the most benefit from section 5:

- Make copies of appendix 2, the compendium of 11 Socratic questions and their attendant follow-on questions.
- For each case study, read and contemplate the role, the scenario, and the assignment.
- On the pages following the role/scenario/assignment,
  - jot down the problem statement,
  - select the top ten questions/follow-on questions you want to ask, and
  - for each question, list those answers that might give you pause.

Case Study #1: Killing the Initiative

16

Your Role

You are the CEO of the Iowa Bar Association, the statewide professional association of lawyers. You have served as CEO for five years, having grown up professionally within the organization, first as a political operative, then as legislative director, then as COO, and finally as CEO when the board's first choice of CEO abruptly departed.

You are not a lawyer but have just recently completed an Executive MBA. You are highly regarded professionally, have a reputation as brilliant and forceful, are quite young for the responsibility, and are married to the CEO of a medium-sized hospital in Des Moines.

You have a fabulous COO and you two have a well-deserved reputation for working superbly together.

The Scenario

A long-standing, miserable relationship between the state's insurance companies and the state bar association recently went from low simmer to full boil when the insurance companies put an initiative on the state ballot. This new law would lower the standard of proof for legal malpractice and allow treble punitive damages for legal malpractice.

It is now February. The initiative will be voted on in November.

While ostensibly designed, in the words of the glossy PR campaign, to protect the hapless public from slick lawyers, the ultimate goal of the initiative is widely believed by insiders to be the weakening of the ability of lawyers to sue insurance companies.

The insurance companies have put together a huge war chest, almost five times the currently available amount in your bank account.

Initial polling indicates that voters are highly supportive of reining in, in the words of the already airing TV spots, "those greedy leeches/lawyers."

The Assignment

In ten days, you will convene a meeting of all the key players at a retreat to map out the plan for defeating the initiative.

You have fenced two hours on your schedule to meet with your COO.

Your goal is to identify the key questions that must be answered at the upcoming retreat.

State the problem

_____
_____
_____
_____

List your top 10 questions and the answers that would give you pause:

Q1: _____
_____
_____

Bad answers to Q1:

_____
_____
_____

Q2: _____
_____
_____

Bad answers to Q2:

_____
_____
_____

Q3: _____
_____
_____

Bad answers to Q3:

_____
_____
_____

Q4: _____

_____

_____

Bad answers to Q4:

_____

_____

_____

Q5: _____

_____

_____

Bad answers to Q5:

_____

_____

_____

Q6: _____

_____

_____

Bad answers to Q6:

_____

_____

_____

Q7: _____

_____

_____

Bad answers to Q7:

_____

_____

_____

Q8: _____

_____

_____

Bad answers to Q8:

_____

_____

_____

Q9: _____

_____

_____

Bad answers to Q9:

_____

_____

_____

Q10: _____

_____

_____

Bad answers to Q10:

_____

_____

_____

My problem statement:

Iowa's lawyers and their clients are in an existential fight at the ballot box in eight months with the state's insurance companies.

If the initiative passes, it will result in a major reduction in the ability of Iowa's citizens to combat rapacious behavior by Iowa's insurance carriers.

My ten key questions:

1. Why is killing this initiative important?
2. Who (plural) speaks for the citizens of Iowa?
3. What do history and best practices tell us about killing an anti-lawyer statewide ballot initiative?
4. Have we done a pre-mortem?
5. Who is going to do what?
6. How will we engage the passions of the hometown lawyers?
7. Can I see the master calendar?
8. How much will it cost?
9. Can I see the budget?
10. What system are we using to track progress?

My discussion

The solution to this problem is in four parts: first, creating a compelling and non-selfserving argument for killing the initiative, then building a coalition, then raising lots of money, and finally running a successful grassroots campaign.

Let's face it, nobody likes lawyers (until you need one). So why would anyone vote *against* something that appears to rein in slimy/greedy lawyers?

The first and most important step is to make sure that there is a compelling argument for Iowa's voters to reject this initiative. And that means making the case that killing the initiative is good for the voters. I would suspect the only group more loathed than lawyers is insurance companies. So as CEO of the bar association, I want to make this about greedy insurance companies making you (the voter) less able to access insurance in general and health insurance in particular. It's really is about crafting the right message.

But simply standing by yourself shouting your message on the street corner is not enough – you need friends. Influential friends. Many friends. Friends who hate insurance companies more than they hate you. And you don't have to look very hard for these friends. The hospitals have to be convinced that this initiative is not in their interests. The patients' rights advocates need to be brought on board. The farmers who need flood and crop insurance also need to jump on your bandwagon. And so on... The CEO knows he cannot go it alone, so getting as many partners on board is critical to success.

The next major hurdle is money. You might win on the merits, but success is not likely if you cannot get your message out. You need every highly paid attorney to contribute. Every law firm needs to be assessed. The hospitals need to be convinced to contribute. The farm cooperatives need to be major public donors. And so on down the line of parties that could feel the impact of the law. It's not pretty, but no money, no message, and no victory.

Finally, the entire Iowa legal ecosystem needs to be an energized force. Your entire team needs to be fired up. The local bar associations need to be fired up. The local lawyers need to be fired up. Every lawn needs a sign. Every farm needs a huge sign next to the freeway. Every voter needs to be contacted. Every chapter of the Rotary Club in the state needs a presentation. If you have a message, and you have money, then the icing on the cake is your ground game. And that means you need a state-wide plan for local success.

Case Study #2: The Pitch of Your Life

Your Role

You are a senior consultant with an elite international consulting firm based in Boston. You have risen rapidly through the ranks in the Strategic Planning practice.

You were born overseas, speak fluent French, German, and Italian, and retired after twenty years in the Foreign Service.

You lead a multi-lingual, multi-cultural team of ten consultants, all with either PhDs or MBAs in International Finance or Strategy. Half of your team is in London, the other half in Boston. Several members of your team are older and nearly all have more years of experience than you as a consultant.

You are married to a brilliant French biochemist who has a strong management background.

The Scenario

You have been tasked with leading the team to create and make the pitch for a major consulting contract with a multinational pharmaceutical based in Switzerland.

Your boss has made it quite clear than she expects an all-out effort on this project, and that if the contract is awarded to the firm, you can expect elevation to partner next year.

The Assignment

You are having dinner with your bride on Saturday evening, and you want to brainstorm about how best to approach this problem.

State the problem

_____
_____
_____
_____

List your top 10 questions and the answers that would give you pause:

Q1 _____
_____
_____

Bad answers to Q1:

_____
_____
_____

Q2: _____
_____
_____

Bad answers to Q2:

_____
_____
_____

Q3: _____
_____
_____

Bad answers to Q3:

_____
_____
_____

Q4: _____

_____

_____

Bad answers to Q4:

_____

_____

_____

Q5: _____

_____

_____

Bad answers to Q5:

_____

_____

_____

Q6: _____

_____

_____

Bad answers to Q6:

_____

_____

_____

Q7: _____

_____

_____

Bad answers to Q7:

_____

_____

_____

Q8: _____

_____

_____

Bad answers to Q8:

_____

_____

_____

Q9: _____

_____

_____

Bad answers to Q9:

_____

_____

_____

Q10: _____

_____

_____

Bad answers to Q10:

_____

_____

_____

My problem statement:

I need to create a passionate and engaged team of near-peers who will work insanely hard over the next three months to prepare for and win a very challenging consulting contract.

My ten key questions:

1. Is the problem statement compelling?
2. What's in it for the members of my consulting team?
3. What do history and best practices tell us?
4. What parts/tools/personnel/monies do we need?
5. Have we "Red Teamed" this solution?
6. Who is going to do what?
7. When are we doing what?
8. How long will it take?
9. What system are we using to track progress?
10. How do we promulgate lessons learned?

My discussion

You are about to ask ten extremely smart and hard-working people to work even harder on a task that may or may not pay off. And the principal beneficiary of success is likely to be you, not them. If you don't find a motivational key, a WIFM for your team members, you will not engage the passion you need to succeed.

There are significant cultural rip currents. You, the leader, are American. Your team is based in London. The client is Swiss, where four languages and cultures – German, French, Italian, and Romansh – compete. You will need to navigate cultures very, very carefully.

This project will benefit immensely from the knowledge base of your own organization and your peers/mentors. You should spend a lot of time upfront to learn how to succeed based on past experience.

Building this pitch will not be cheap. How will you make sure you have the financial and resource support you need to make sure it gets done right?

Consulting firms are often hotbeds of competition. If you are up for partner, how will you get the help you need from peers to effectively "Red Team" your pitch? How will you avoid sabotage?

Odds are high your team already has full plates. How will you parse the workloads so you don't run your team into the ground?

Finally, does this proposal have a chance for success, or are you simply spinning your wheels? Many consulting contracts are preordained and opening the floor for competing bids is merely an exercise – the game can be rigged. You need to have a long and difficult conversation with your boss to make sure that if the bid fails, that you are not professionally harmed.

Case Study #3: We're Moving to Albuquerque!

18

Your Role

You are the CEO of one of New Mexico's largest not-for-profits, based in the state capital, Santa Fe.

The Scenario

You have occupied your headquarters building for more than a century. Unfortunately, that historical building is falling apart and will need a large cash infusion to remain viable as your headquarters.

With the full concurrence of the board, you have sold the building to a historical preservation charity for a rather large windfall profit. The terms of the contract allow you to remain in the building, but at the end of an eighteen-month term, you must be completely gone.

Your board has directed you to take the sale proceeds and move the organization into a shiny new building in the state's largest city, Albuquerque. Almost your entire experienced and loyal staff of thirty-five are domiciled in Santa Fe, which is about an hour from Albuquerque.

Your board chair is the CEO of one of Albuquerque's most innovative high-techs, and you have a fabulous and trustworthy working relationship with her. Your extremely competent COO has been with the company for twenty-five years, is steeped in the lore and background of the organization, and is well regarded and trusted by the team. She lives five minutes from the old building, her children are in the Santa Fe school system, and her husband is the chief of staff of the Assembly speaker.

The Assignment

You have asked for and received two hours on the Board Chair's calendar to chat about the next steps.

To prepare for this critical meeting, you need to create a problem statement and a list of the key questions you want to discuss with her.

State the problem

_____

_____

_____

_____

List your top 10 questions and the answers that would give you pause:

Q1: _____

_____

_____

Bad answers to Q1:

_____

_____

_____

Q2: _____

_____

_____

Bad answers to Q2:

_____

_____

_____

Q3: _____

_____

_____

Bad answers to Q3:

_____

_____

_____

Q4: _____

_____

_____

Bad answers to Q4:

_____

_____

_____

Q5: _____

_____

_____

Bad answers to Q5:

_____

_____

_____

Q6: _____

_____

_____

Bad answers to Q6:

_____

_____

_____

Q7: _____

_____

_____

Bad answers to Q7:

_____

_____

_____

Q8: _____
_____
_____

Bad answers to Q8:
_____
_____
_____

Q9: _____
_____
_____

Bad answers to Q9:
_____
_____
_____

Q10: _____
_____
_____

Bad answers to Q10:
_____
_____
_____

My problem statement:

The organization is faced with a difficult choice: stay at the center of political power, Santa Fe, or move to the center of economic power, Albuquerque. The choice must be very carefully and thoughtfully made so it optimizes the long-term health of the organization.

My ten key questions:

1. Why are we really moving to Albuquerque?
2. Can the organization survive the potential loss of many key team members, including the COO?
3. Have all the stakeholders been identified?
4. Have all the stakeholders opined?
5. Have all the stakeholders concurred?
6. How are we going to solve the problem?
7. Where are we doing what?
8. When are we doing what?
9. How long will it take?
10. How much will it cost?

My discussion

This case study is about two very distinct issues – first, clearly thinking through and debating the reason for uprooting the entire organization from the state capital to the state's economic center of gravity, and then second, implementing the decision.

It is clear to you, and everyone else, that the move from Santa Fe to Albuquerque would be highly disruptive. This should stimulate a number of lines of questioning:

- What is the rationale for moving to Albuquerque in the first place? Does the fundamental decision make sense?
- Are there advantages to "cleaning house" (anticipating that many of your team will leave if forced to move to Albuquerque) and bringing in a whole new team?

    o   Do the advantages outweigh the disadvantages?

    o   Is there a third path – keeping a small team in Santa Fe and the larger team in Albuquerque?

This difficult choice should be made with a very expansive mindset. All choices and options, even some highly creative and unconventional ones, should be explored.

This decision is about much more than geography! This would be a great time to conduct a sensing and visioning exercise to line up what the board and management believe the organization should look like in five and fifteen years, and how the choice of headquarters location plays into that vision.

The actual "where is the building going to go" and "how will we move there" is important, but they are really second-order questions that could be outsourced.

Case Study #4: Where Are We Going for the Honeymoon, Dear?

19

Your Role

You are getting married to the man of your dreams in twelve months.

You have known each other for more than a decade, since you were both undergraduates at Yale. You spent five years after college in the Army Corps of Engineers, most of it deployed overseas to the Middle and Near East. You are highly organized and efficient, and are now COO of a biotech start-up with an IPO probable in the next eighteen months.

Your spouse-to-be is a trial lawyer who graduated from Yale Law. He just made partner at a high-powered boutique firm at the tender age of thirty-two. He has at least two major cases in the next six months. Your spouse was born into a Texas minister's family and is extremely thrifty. You grew up in an affluent East Coast family.

After spending the five years post-graduation apart, you now reside together in Austin, Texas. There are no children in the past, present, or future.

You intend a very small intimate wedding, but you both really want a six-week blowout honeymoon.

The Scenario

You and your spouse both work a minimum of sixty-hour weeks.

Because you have extensive management experience as a COO, you have become the *de facto* honeymoon and wedding planner. The wedding is on autopilot, but no honeymoon decisions of any kind have been made.

You are now one year out from the honeymoon.

The Assignment

You and your spouse-to-be have booked a weekend at a rustic cabin in the Texas Hill Country.

He knows that you intend to discuss the honeymoon, so you want to be prepared with a list of key questions to ask and jointly answer.

You have fenced an hour at your favorite watering hole with your best friend to come up with the list.

State the problem

_____

_____

_____

_____

List your top 10 questions and the answers that would give you pause:

Q1: _____

_____

_____

Bad answers to Q1:

_____

_____

_____

Q2: _____

_____

_____

Bad answers to Q2:

_____

_____

_____

Q3: _____

_____

_____

Bad answers to Q3:

_____

_____

_____

Q4: _____
_____
_____

Bad answers to Q4:
_____
_____
_____

Q5: _____
_____
_____

Bad answers to Q5:
_____
_____
_____

Q6: _____
_____
_____

Bad answers to Q6:
_____
_____
_____

Q7: _____
_____
_____

Bad answers to Q7:
_____
_____
_____

Q8: _____

_____

_____

Bad answers to Q8:

_____

_____

_____

Q9: _____

_____

_____

Bad answers to Q9:

_____

_____

_____

Q10: _____

_____

_____

Bad answers to Q10:

_____

_____

_____

My problem statement:
We want to have a great honeymoon that reflects who we are and what we want to remember about the start of our married life.

My ten key questions:
1. Honey, what would you like to do on our honeymoon?
2. Where would you like to go on our honeymoon, dear?
3. When are we going to be able to fit in the honeymoon of our dreams?
4. How will the weather affect our honeymoon?
5. How will the politics of a given location impact our honeymoon?
6. Who is going to do what?
7. What tasks are we outsourcing?
8. How much will it cost?
9. Can I see the budget?
10. What do history and best practices tell us?

Discussion
This problem is about getting the couple to identify their wants. It's not an implementation question. And the hard part is nailing down the spouse, both in getting his opinion and his participation.

Money and time are clearly going to be bones of contention. Money because the fiscal values of the couple are different, and time because of their heavy external commitments.

Perhaps an extended honeymoon might not be realistic.

But talking the issue through is really one of the first tests for this marriage!

I included this non-work example to emphasize the point that the techniques of crafting a problem statement and then asking (and answering) great Socratic questions are also applicable to your personal life.

GREAT MANAGERIAL TRAITS

I believe great managers display seven invaluable *traits*:

- o They ask questions well.
- o They are both courageous and honest.
- o They are principled in their flexibility, skepticism, and optimism.
- o They listen to and talk to themselves.
- o They connect leadership and management.
- o They simplify.
- o They manage by *asking* around.

Earlier in the book, I presented the questions you ask of others.

This next section is about asking yourself whether you are exhibiting these seven traits.

Asking Questions Well

20

Am I asking questions well?

This book is all about asking great questions. Sections 2, 3, and 4 focus on helping managers ask great questions of others.

But it's not *just* about asking great questions. Because it's so easy to ask great questions badly, great managers need to learn to ask questions well.

> **Great managers ask great questions well.**

Use a spirit of inquiry

It's easy to ask questions in a hostile or insinuating tone. In the book *Difficult Conversations – How to Discuss What Matters Most*, Douglas Stone breaks down any conversation into three separate components: the facts, the feelings, and the ego conversations. And he further analyzes the conversation about facts into three opportunities for failure: arguing about the veracity of the facts, arguing about the intentions of the participants, and arguing about the blame to be assigned.

All of us have started a question-answer session that quickly degraded into hostility and anger by arguing about the veracity, the intentions, or the blame.

Since the focus of this book is on asking great questions, it's critically important to ask the great questions in a way that does not engender hostility and anger.

Ask questions in a way that does not engender hostility and anger.

Dr. Jim Hay, one of my mentors, would preface any tough question, and he was not shy about asking really hard questions, with the phrase "Help me understand." And he really did want to understand – it was not *pro forma*. Dr. Hay's delivery was likewise designed to reduce, rather than inflame, tension. He always spoke with a thoughtful mien and kind tone. He never flinched from tough questions, but you never felt bad about him asking.

That's the reputation you want to strive for.

Ask the second-order question

Another early learning occurred when I was tasked, as a junior officer, to visit a ship captained by a very senior and very blunt officer. I was to determine the status of a repair to a mission-critical antenna.

It was not a pleasant interaction. Having been brought up with Teutonic directness, I came right out and asked him whether the crew had fixed the antenna. Ask a simple question, get a simple answer. Wrong.

By asking the question directly in a crowd, I had publicly impugned his managerial skills, and I found myself inside the verbal blast zone, as he very candidly and very loudly informed me that "Of course they fixed the antenna, did I (Tom) think they were slovenly or sloppy?" The actual phrasing was peppered with a number of unprintable expletives.

Later, my boss suggested a different, more tactful approach to asking questions. Rather than come right out and ask the obvious (and perhaps insulting) direct question, don't ask the obvious question.

Assume the answer to the obvious question is affirmative. Then ask the indirect second-order question. The trick is to ask a follow-on question that implies the answer to the first question is in the affirmative. And toss in an offer to help!

> **Ask a question that implies the answer to the unasked but obvious first question is in the affirmative.**

Rather than ask the direct "Is the antenna fixed?" ask the indirect "Did your team have any problems on the retest for the antenna that we could help with?"

If the answer to the first-order question is negative, it allows the person being asked a bit of verbal wiggle room, particularly if the question is asked in public.

Be unfailingly positive, polite, and self-deprecating

Smile. Be positive. Be polite. Assume you don't know everything.

> **Smile. Be positive. Be polite. Assume you don't know everything.**

Easy to do, and can make answering your tough questions less painful.

Remember that people are afraid of you, since you read this book and now have a reputation for asking hard questions, and no one likes to be embarrassed.

Screaming or yelling or being an arrogant ass is not a long-term strategy for success. Or even a short-term strategy for success.

Be like Dr. Jim Hay – thoughtful, kind, and yet unrelenting.

Dealing with 3 percent or 2 percent - Show me!

Earlier I proposed that some fraction of the population is either misdemeanor dumb or felony stupid or sociopathic (see chapter 14). Unlike the other 95 percent who are highly likely to be trustworthy, the 2 percent/3 percent are likely to prevaricate or obfuscate.

When dealing with the stupid or malicious, don't take their word for much of anything, have them prove it. Use the old Missouri adage "Show me."

And then find a way to move the stupid and malicious out of your world.

Use every question as a teachable moment

The essence of the Socratic method is using questions to teach. A great manager is a great teacher.

In the pursuit of answers and in the pursuit of managing the solution to a problem, don't forget to invest the time in your people by helping them become better managers.

Great managers consider everyone working with them to be a great manager-in-training.

Take the opportunity to explain why you asked the question. Take the opportunity to show them how they can emulate your

My second-to-last question is always "What have I forgotten to ask you?"

Socratic Management Paradigm with their team. Expand their thinking.

I dedicated this book to my five greatest management teachers. I hope that you will someday be perceived as a great management teacher, so use every question as a teachable moment.

My last question is always "What help do you need from me?"

What have I forgotten to ask you?

The second-to-last question I ask in a managerial interaction is designed to tease out that which I was not smart enough to ask. "What have I forgotten to ask you?" or "What else do I need to know?" presumes that you don't know all the questions to ask.

It creates an opportunity to let people shine – by demonstrating that there is stuff they know that you don't.

How can I help you?

The last question I always ask is "What help do you need from me?"

Assuming the question is not asked *pro forma* or in a tone of bored rote, then it closes out the conversation on a positive note.

And if you are asked for something, deliver.

CHAPTER SUMMARY

- Ask the great questions in a way that does not engender hostility and anger.
- Preface any tough question with the words "help me understand."
- Ask the indirect second-order question. Ask a follow-on question that implies the answer to the first is in the affirmative.
- Smile. Be positive. Be polite.
- Assume you don't know everything.
- When dealing with the stupid or the malicious, use "Show me."
- Every question is a teachable moment.
- Ask what you've forgotten to ask.
- Close by asking how you can help.

Honesty and Courage

21

Am I being honest and courageous?

Honesty and courage are the two indispensable traits of great managers (and great leaders).

Courage and honesty are inextricably linked. You cannot be a dishonest great manager, and managers without moral courage are doomed.

Honesty

Lack of integrity (and I use honesty and integrity interchangeably) manifests itself from two perspectives – personal dishonesty and managerial dishonesty.

Lack of personal integrity is relatively easy to spot. The line you cross is usually very clear. For example, thou shall not lie, cheat, or steal. Crossing the line(s) is sometimes hard to avoid in a temptation-filled world, but the lines are nonetheless clear.

And once exposed, personal dishonesty and getting fired are usually found close together.

The line that defines managerial integrity is much more difficult to spot. In fact, managerial dishonesty usually manifests itself by inaction.

Managerial dishonesty usually manifests itself by inaction.

After retiring as CEO, I was asked to become the Interim Executive Director for an initiative that held great promise for our region. Everyone wanted the initiative to succeed. But try as we might, we could not get the various constituents – stakeholders, really – to put aside their parochial self-interests for the greater good.

It became obvious the initiative was failing, and that we would have to invest money that we did not have and were not likely to get. Rather than hanging on and hoping for a miracle, I recommended, because it was the right thing to do, to terminate the effort. I wanted so much to succeed, but it just was not going to happen.

Managerial integrity was about facing the facts and recommending the termination of the initiative to the board.

Managerial *honesty* is all about *recognizing* what's right.

The board, when presented with the unvarnished truth, reluctantly but unanimously concurred.

> **Managerial *honesty* is all about *recognizing* what's right.**

Courage

Courage, in the managerial context, is not about charging forward into a hail of bullets. Management *courage* is about *doing* the right thing even (and particularly) when it's hard.

It means saying no when everyone is saying yes. It means saying yes when everyone is saying no.

> **Management *courage* is about *doing* the right thing even (and particularly) when it's hard.**

Saying no when everyone is saying yes

When you recognize that something that is at best wrong and at worst insidious, you have to have the guts to say, "No, we're not going to do that." You have to learn to say no when everyone is saying yes.

> **You have to learn to say *no* when everyone is saying *yes*.**

Parking. Seriously, there is courage in parking? Yup. So on *McKee*, the submarine tender I was second in command of, we had a four-month maintenance period at a civilian shipyard in San Diego. While most of San Diego is a delightful, safe, and friendly place, this particular locale was none of the above. In fact, it was downright scary after dark. All the senior folks had reserved pierside parking spots. No sweat for the brass. The other 1,400 less privileged sailors had to park their cars, if they were lucky enough to find a spot, then walk a long way through a very dodgy neighborhood. When we complained, the answer was "Tough, everyone else has been doing it." Oh, and over a third of the crew were women — who would have had to walk through a neighborhood you would never want your daughter going through alone.

Nope, we're not going to do that.

First, we laid down the law: no walking alone or even in groups through the dodgy neighborhood. Period. Ever. No parking in the dodgy neighborhood. Period. Ever.

Then, we organized, staffed, and paid for our own shuttle service that ran on-demand twenty-four hours a day from a safe, well-lit remote parking site. And we staffed the parking lot with burly masters-at-arms.

And if the bus was late, that was on us, not the sailor.

And not one person was hurt and no cars were damaged.

Sometimes you have to have the courage to say no!

Saying yes when everyone is saying no

You have to learn to say yes when everyone is saying no. When everyone is saying no to something that is clearly right,

> **You have to learn to say *yes* when everyone is saying *no*.**

you have to have the courage to say, "Yes, we're going to do that."

It's the little things that show your true colors.

The phone call went something like this: "Hey, Mr. CEO, your guys completely gooned up my portrait in the San Diego physician directory!" And this was not in a happy voice.

A little background. Annually at Medical Society we collected every doctor's input, including their treasured self-image, and published a directory that included that photo. The directory went online and in hard copy to the entire healthcare community in San Diego.

The irate physician had just had a professional photo taken that made her look fabulous. We published the previous year's photo, which was much less fabulous.

This doctor had been a dues-paying member of the society for more than twenty years.

My answer was to her was simple. First, we're going to refund your annual dues. You fly free for a year. It didn't matter whose fault it was, we're taking responsibility. Second, we're going to immediately fix the digital edition. Finally, we're going to send out an *errata* page for this (and one other) error to the same people who got the original version.

My staff was aghast. "That's a lot of money, Mr. CEO!" And by the way, they pointed out with some frustration, turns out the physician in question had sent in the new photograph late. To the wrong person. "It really wasn't our fault," said my staff.

Yup, but it's the right thing to do for a loyal long-time member.

Sometimes, you have to say yes when everyone wants to say no.

The ghost of Norman Schwarzkopf

General Norman Schwarzkopf, the architect of Desert Storm 1, was often quoted as saying, "Knowing the right thing to do is easy. Doing the right thing is hard."

Honesty is knowing the right answer is really the right answer.

Courage is doing something about it.

Great managers have to do both.

CHAPTER SUMMARY

- You cannot be a dishonest great manager.
- You cannot be a cowardly great manager.
- Lack of integrity manifests itself in two perspectives: personal dishonesty and managerial dishonesty.
- You have to learn to say no when everyone is saying yes.
- You have to learn to say yes when everyone is saying no.

Principled Flexibility, Skepticism, and Optimism

Am I being principled?

There are as many great principles as there are great managers.

Know your principles, values, and ethics, and constantly check yourself to see whether you are living up to them.

What are *your* principles, values, and ethics?

The only two wrong answers to that question are these: "I don't know what my principles, values, and ethics are" and "I have not written down my principles, values, and ethics."

After that, there are as many right answers as there are people.

So know your principles, values, and ethics, and be prepared to articulate them. From memory. At the drop of a hat. As a teachable moment, anytime.

And live your principles, values, and ethics — demonstrate them through your words and behavior. All the time. Even when no one is looking. Particularly when no one is looking.

> Live your principles, values, and ethics. Even when no one is looking.

Sharing three of my principles

I have three principles that I believe are common to every great manager. They are:

✓ principled flexibility – how you change your mind,

✓ principled skepticism – how you deal with a situation that is not to your liking,

✓ principled positivity – how you deal with adversity.

Principled flexibility, not flip-flopping

You're going to change your mind. It's the nature of a dynamic world.

Changing your mind is not a bad thing. Flip-flopping is a bad thing. The differences between a flip-flopper and a great manager are the following:

The great manager explains why she changed her mind. If there is a rational case for the modification, then everyone can and should understand it.

The great manager consults with her team, except in a real emergency where there is no time and a rapid decision is imperative[25]. If you ask your team their opinion, they are much more likely to support a decision, even if it's not what they like.

And most importantly, the change does not compromise a principle, a value, or an ethic. You can be flexible about almost everything, but not your principles, values, and ethics.

That's why I call it principled flexibility.

In fact, principles, values, or ethics ought to drive change. If you are not operating in alignment with them, then change direction. Reread the previous chapter on courage and integrity!

Principled skepticism, not whining

It's human nature to complain. We naturally question authority, question our leaders, question our structures. We love to complain!

---

25 The number of times that an immediate decision is required should be a ridiculously small fraction of your decisions – and then you should assess why you got into that predicament. Quick-draw decisions do not have a good track record!

Dr. Chris Kane, the CEO of the University of California San Diego Health Physicians, leads more than 1,400 doctors at a prestigious academic medical center. He preaches a rigor to complaining that takes skepticism far beyond the usual daily griping.

If you are data-driven, reality-based, and thoughtful about your skepticism, then you are a principled skeptic.

The converse is also true. If you are not data-driven, not reality-based, or not thoughtful, then you are a whiner.

Become data-driven, reality-based, and thoughtful about your skepticism.

There is a wonderful scene in the 1998 movie *Saving Private Ryan* where Tom Hanks' World War Two character, Captain Miller, is asked by one of his terribly frustrated Rangers about why the Captain doesn't gripe when they are sent on a dangerous wild goose chase across a Norman countryside swarming with hostile Germans. Captain Miller responds that he doesn't gripe to his troopers; he only complains to his boss. And he really doesn't do that either.

Great managers are principled and rational skeptics – life is tough, yes, but difficulties need to be seen neither through rose-colored glasses nor through the dark glasses of negativity, but rather through the lenses of data, thoughtful consideration, and reality.

I hate messing with Information Technology (IT). If IT works, don't mess with it, because change is so darn painful. After years on an antiquated system – obsolescent hardware, unsupported software, and unreliable data – I bit the bullet as CEO of the Medical Society and made the strategic decision to get into the twenty-first century. And it was more of a necessity than a luxury.

The whining and complaining started immediately. The team was professionally terrified about the change. "We won't know how to do anything," "We'll have to relearn everything," "What happens if," "It'll never work."

How to shift from whining to principled and rational skepticism?

First, we developed a detailed, data-rich plan that answered all of the first nine questions of this book. And rather than stifling the complaining, I channeled it. For example, if we have to re-learn everything, could we set aside a week where we close the office and just focus on learning the new system? "Great idea, yup, done," said the CEO.

Second, we became *uber*-disciplined about reality. No, the world was not going to end. No, we were not going back to punch cards. Every wildly irrational fear was met with a dose of rational reality. And in the process of discussing some ostensibly "irrational" fears, we discovered not a few steps that would improve the odds of success. It sounded a lot like a pre-mortem! We harnessed our fears to create better answers.

Finally, we forced ourselves to be thoughtful. How? By studying history for lessons learned, by taking the time to think and speculate intelligently, by the manager (myself) remaining calm and positive (see the next heading) at all times.

Rational skepticism – data-driven, reality-based, and thoughtful – got us through. Not without problems, but with the problems under control.

Rational skepticism is not a panacea, but it sure beats the alternative. And it should be one of the core principles of great managers.

Principled positivity

No one likes working for or with a grouch.

Great managers have a sunny outlook on the project and life. Principled positivity is about finding a way, even if it's tough, to be optimistic and humorous. You'll feel better, and so will your team!

In early summer 1805, Captain Meriwether Lewis climbed out of the Missouri River bottoms near present-day Fergus, Montana, and first espied the snow-covered Rockies way, way

Principled positivity is about finding a way, even if it's tough, to be optimistic and humorous.

off in the distance – mountains he and his team had to cross in late fall or early winter in order to reach the Pacific.

President Thomas Jefferson had just purchased, sight unseen, one-third of the North American continent, and needed someone to walk the property. He asked Lewis, his personal secretary, to explore and to map from St. Louis to the Pacific Ocean and back.

With no clue about the route to the Pacific, Lewis and his co-leader, William Clark, marched off smartly from St. Louis in 1804 with his black lab, Seaman; thirty-two volunteers; a French Canadian trapper named Charbonneau; and the trapper's sixteen-year-old Shoshone wife, Sacajawea, the interpreter for the expedition.

Here is what Lewis wrote on May 26, 1805: "I beheld the Rocky Mountains for the first time covered in snow, with the sun shining in such a manner as to give me the most plain and satisfactory view. While I viewed these mountains, I felt a secret pleasure in finding myself near the head of the heretofore conceived boundless Missouri. But, when I reflect on those difficulties which this snowy barrier would most probably throw in my way to the Pacific, and the sufferings and hardships of myself and party in them, it in some way counterbalanced the joy I felt in the first moments in which I gazed on them."

He knew what was coming, it was not likely to be easy, and it wasn't. Author Stephen Ambrose perfectly titled his history of the Lewis and Clark expedition *Undaunted Courage*.

Lewis continued, "But as I have always held it a crime to anticipate evils, I will believe it a good comfortable road until I'm compelled to believe differently."

Principled positivity in action!

Lewis led the Corps of Discovery over 8,000 uncharted miles in three years, and lost one man (to appendicitis). Incredible!

> **But as I have always held it a crime to anticipate evils, I will believe it a good and comfortable road until I'm compelled to believe differently.**

And if you want another example of undaunted courage and principled positivity, Sacajawea gave birth to her first child half-way through the expedition, and uncomplainingly carried her son for the remaining 4,000 miles.

So when you see your version of the snowy Rockies with no idea of how to cross the barrier, think about the principled positivity of Meriwether Lewis and Sacajawea, and let their example inspire you.

Paraphrasing former Chairman of the Joint Chiefs, General Colin Powell, "positivity is a force multiplier."

Positivity is a force multiplier.

CHAPTER SUMMARY

- You're going to change your mind – it's normal.
- Great managers do three things when they change their mind:
    - ✓ Explain the reasoning,
    - ✓ Consult with their team,
    - ✓ Never compromise a value or an ethic.
- Know your principles, values, and ethics, and be prepared to articulate them.
- Live your values and ethics in your behavior.
- Be a principled and rational skeptic:
    - ✓ Data-driven,
    - ✓ Reality-based, and
    - ✓ Thoughtful about your skepticism.
- Principled positivity is about finding a way, even if it's tough, to be optimistic and humorous.
- Difficulties need to be seen neither through rose-colored glasses nor through the dark glasses of negativity.
- Positivity is a force multiplier.

Listening to and Talking to Yourself

Am I listening and talking to myself?

Great managers talk to themselves. Perhaps not out loud, but they constantly remind themselves of what truly matters.

Great managers also listen to themselves. When the voice in their head starts to speak, often in whispers, they listen very carefully.

Talking to yourself

A manager will make a lot of decisions. Hundreds, even thousands, a year. It's very easy to lose sight of your principles when you're making so many decisions.

I developed two verbal touchstones when the going got tough. These two questions sound the same, but they are not. The first question is technical, and the second is about values.

Is this the correct thing to do?

When I had a difficult call to make, I would say, out loud, sometimes in private, and often in public, "What's the right thing to do here?"

What's the right thing to do here?

First, it contextualized the decision-making process. Had we done everything to make the best possible technical decision?

Second, it allowed the team to weigh in – maybe I had missed something.

Finally, it helped me make the sometimes-difficult leap from easy and wrong, to difficult and right (see chapter 21 on the topics of honesty and courage).

Does it reflect our values?

When people brought me a proposed decision, I would ask out loud, sometimes in private, and often in public, "Is this legal, moral, and ethical?"

> **Is this legal, moral, and ethical?**

I did this for three reasons.

First, it reflected that I wanted to do the right thing right. Because I had articulated my guiding principles in writing, my team and I knew what the "right thing done right" was.

Second, it allowed anyone within listening range to weigh in if this proposed decision was a little dicey.

Finally, it forced me to make absolutely sure that not only was the decision technically correct but that the decision was morally correct. More often than I would like to admit, a technically correct choice was morally or ethically dicey or worse. Asking the question out loud helped me stay on the moral track.

Listening to yourself

Not only do you need to talk to yourself, you need to also listen to yourself.

It's been said that there are no surprised managers, only managers who didn't see or who didn't listen.

> **There are no surprised managers, only managers who didn't see or who didn't listen.**

When something bad happens, unless it's a real (and extremely rare) Black Swan event (see chapter 8), you almost certainly had an inkling. Prior to the disaster, deep in your brain or soul or your consciousness, you felt that something just wasn't right. And you ignore it at your peril.

One example stands out in my mind. On *McKee*, we had a mixed-gender crew of more than 1,500. Most every week I would spend an hour or so adjudicating various misdemeanor behaviors – normal Navy stuff.

The alleged miscreants would present themselves, our lawyer would outline the charges, the chain of command would opine, and I eventually made a choice: send the case up to the Captain, who held legal authority, for a full-blown judicial event, or dismiss the case.

One day almost thirty years ago, a young female Petty Officer stood at attention in front of me in her dress whites, accused of going absent without leave (AWOL). In context, going AWOL is one of the more egregious of the offenses I saw.

As I looked in her service jacket, I noted her excellent performance on *McKee* and a prior ship.

She had freely admitted to going AWOL. The facts of her offense were not in question. But I wanted to get to the *why*. As I usually did, I asked her to tell her story.

Not a word. She stared fixedly at the bulkhead behind me. No eye contact. I persisted, with the same result. Not a word. And she was starting to crack.

My alarm bells were going off. Great performer, admits to going AWOL, no reason or explanation, sailor about to meltdown .... Something was very wrong here.

I did something very unusual for these kinds of proceedings: I cleared my cabin, asked her to sit down, and spoke with her one-on-one. It took me almost ten minutes to get her story out, and it was ugly. She had been systematically sexually harassed for months by her chain of command. She went AWOL because she had no one to talk to and she just couldn't take it anymore.

I was flabbergasted, embarrassed, and infuriated.

Flabbergasted because I had no idea the cancer of sexual harassment had metastasized onto *McKee*. Embarrassed because it had happened on my watch. And infuriated that her chain of command had participated in it, abetted it, or both.

I dismissed her case on the spot. She was free to go. We held the chain of command accountable. And I began a years-long mission to root out the cancer.

All because I listened to that voice in my head telling me something's not right here. When something feels wrong, it probably is.

So listen to your instincts and talk to yourself.

> **When something feels wrong, it probably is.**

CHAPTER SUMMARY

- It's very easy to lose sight of your principles when you're making many decisions.
- Frequently ask,
    - ✓ "What's the right thing to do here?"
    - ✓ "Is this legal, moral, and ethical?"
- There are no surprised managers, only managers who didn't see or who didn't listen.
- When something feels wrong, it probably is.

Connecting Leadership and Management

Am I connecting management and leadership?

Management cannot occur in the absence of leadership.

Sometimes the manager is also the leader, and sometimes not. But in either case, a great manager must understand what a great leader does – and does not do.

In 2018, I described a paradigm for leadership in my first book, *7 Roles Great Leaders Don't Delegate.* The key concept is that great *leaders* focus on a vital few roles, and delegate everything else. Those seven unique roles were sensing, visioning, accultura-tion, enabling, deciding, embracing responsibility, and mentoring.

> **Great *leaders* focus on a vital few roles, and delegate everything else**

In this book, I present a paradigm for management that involves asking 11 questions, with the attendant follow-on or ancillary questions. The great *manager* asks questions, has a strong sense of what the answers should not look like, and then Socratically points his team in the right direction.

> **The great *manager* asks questions, has a strong sense of what the answers should not look like, and then Socratically points his team in the right direction**

In chapter 2, I differentiated leadership and management.

However, there are strong connections between the leadership model in my first book and the management model in this book.

7 Roles Great Leaders Don't Delegate

Briefly, here are the seven roles I believe are not delegable, posed in the form of questions:

- Sensing—how do you develop a clear strategic picture of today's reality?
- Visioning—how do you craft a path to a desirable tomorrow?
- Acculturation—how do you mold the organizational and individual behaviors necessary to achieve the vision?
- Enabling—how do you ensure your team has the tools to achieve the vision?
- Deciding—how do you make decisions that achieve the vision and are consistent with the culture?
- Owning—how do you establish ownership and responsibility?
- Mentoring—how do you find and teach the next generation of leaders?

The leadership roles "Sensing" and "Visioning" are connected to three managerial questions – "Why?" "What?" and "For Whom?"

Sensing is gathering, from many disparate internal and external sources, the data necessary to create a mental model of the organization in the environment in which that organization operates.

Visioning is using the strategic picture created from sensing to create a vision of the future.

Strategizing takes the vision, the principles, the mission, and the environment to create the attendant dynamic strategies.

The answer to the managerial question "Why?" should come directly from the vision.

The answer to the managerial questions "What?" and "For Whom?" should come directly from the strategy.

The leadership roles "Acculturation" and "Enabling" are connected to four managerial questions: "How?" "Who?" "How Long?" and "How Much?"

The leader sets and owns the culture of the organization, and provides his team with all the tools necessary to implement the vision.

Enabling involves people, priority, money, tools, knowledge, and process.

Of the six Socratic management questions connected to generating a solution to the problem, four are connected directly to culture and enabling.

The leadership roles Acculturation and Enabling must occur in order to answer the managerial questions: "How?", "Who?", "How Long?" and "How Much?"

The leadership role "Mentoring" is connected to the managerial question "How are we learning?"

The leader selects, trains, and mentors the next generation of leaders.

And mentoring ties directly into the managerial question "How are we learning?"

Keeping Leadership and Management Distinct

You cannot divorce leadership and management. They are inextricably intertwined. And dramatically different.

If you have great leadership and poor management, you have energetic chaos.

If you have poor leaders and great managers, then you have a well-run but directionless bureaucracy.

The goal is to strive for great leadership and management.

F. Scott Fitzgerald said "...the test of a first-rate intelligence is the ability to hold two opposed ideas in mind at the same time and still retain the ability to function."

And only the truly exceptional person can *naturally* both lead and manage.

For those who are not blessed with this extraordinary dual gift, I wrote these two books so that you have a paradigm for both leadership and management, know how they are connected, and also know how they are not.

CHAPTER SUMMARY

- Management cannot occur in the absence of leadership.
- The answer to the question "Why?" should come directly from the vision.
- The answer to the questions "What? and "For Whom?" should come directly from the strategy.
- Acculturation and enabling must occur to answer "How, Who, How Much, and How Long?"
- Mentoring ties directly into the "How are we learning?" question.
- Leadership and management are inextricably intertwined, yet separate.

Simplify

25

Am I simplifying?

We live in a complex and complicated world. Everything is connected to everything else. We cannot see all the wheels and levers behind the curtain. We are deluged in fact, fiction, and fantasy.

You are not going to change the world, and *you* have to adapt to it.

But are you managing the project as simply as possible?

Make it simple

The world may be complex, but great managers reduce complexity to simplicity *for their teams*.

Mark Twain famously said, on the matter of brevity, "I didn't have time to write a short letter, so I wrote a long one instead."

When in doubt, choose simplicity and brevity.

> The world may be complex, but great managers reduce complexity to simplicity *for their teams*.

Most people (including you) can do only one thing at a time

It's a sad fact that, despite all the hype and the excitement about productivity-improving gizmos, you are still a human being, wired to do one thing at a time.

I chuckle at my Gen Z son's desk, where yesterday he had a desktop screen, two laptops, and his cell phone all up and running different software. *But he could still only look at one screen at a time.*

He can shift between screens much more rapidly than I can, his reflexes and reaction times are way faster than mine, but he can still only look at and process one task at a time.

I map my days out with precision to accomplish as much as possible – but I can still work on only one job at a time.

And so it is with your people.

You, the manager, can plan more than one job at a time. However, the workers can still only accomplish one task at a time.

Managing in the age of complexity

Your job as a manager in today's world is to make it simple for your people. *You* still have to appreciate and understand the complexity raging outside your team's door.

But the team you manage has to be shielded from the whirling storm, and they have to *focus.*

As CEO of the Medical Society, I was involved in several intense political struggles with groups inimical to the interests of San Diego's physicians. There were meetings after meetings discussing the intricacies of strategy and tactics. As the manager, I had to buffer my team from the multiple and fluctuating demands on their time. I had to provide my team consistency and focus in the face of everyone having a "better" idea on how they should be spending their time.

Some guy named Occam

In the thirteenth century, the English Franciscan friar William of Ockham (now usually spelled Occam) developed a religious idea that has morphed into the secular statement, "The simplest solution is most likely the right one."

Occam's Razor, a varia-
tion on that idea, is a way of
choosing between competing

> **The simplest solution is most likely the right one.**

hypotheses that make the same predictions. It states that *one should select the solution with the fewest assumptions*[26].

Keep Occam's Razor handy!

Some guy named Murphy

Every manager learns early on that, quoting the irascible and apocryphal Murphy, "Anything that can go wrong, will. At the worst possible time."

In my workshop, I have a full page of the corollaries to Murphy's Law. They range from the humorous to the tragic. I have to periodically review them to keep from doing something stupid!

But the best defenses against revalidating Murphy's Law or its

corollaries are common sense and simplicity. Because simple plans are typically more robust in the face of Murphy's Law.

> **Simple plans are typically more robust in the face of Murphy's Law.**

Keep Murphy out of your world!

Keep it simple, short (KISS)

'Nuff said.

---

26 It is not meant to be a way of choosing between hypotheses that make different predictions.

CHAPTER SUMMARY

- You can do only one thing at a time.
- Keep Occam's Razor handy.
- Avoid revalidating Murphy's Law.
- Keep it simple, short. (KISS)

Manage
by Asking
Around

26

Manage by Walking Around

Many managers were taught early on to manage by walking around (MBWA). [27]

In this penultimate chapter, I want to introduce a new concept that riffs on MBWA.

I loved walking around my spaces. First, it got me out of the office and disconnected from the phone. Sometimes, just to keep that disconnection, I would leave my cell phone in my executive assistant's hand, with clear instructions to let the caller know I was indisposed!

Second, it gave me the opportunity to chat with my team, who, in addition to being nice people, were the linchpins to the success of my organization.

Third, it got me away from my groaning desk, piled high with stuff to do. Escapism, if you will.

---

[27] BusinessDictionary.com defines MBWA as a style ... which involves managers wandering around, in an unstructured manner, through the workplace(s), at random, to check with employees, equipment, or on the status of ongoing work. The emphasis is on the word *wandering* as an unplanned movement within a workplace, rather than a plan where employees expect a visit from managers at more systematic, preapproved, or scheduled times.

Manage by Asking Around

Later in my time as CEO, I conceptualized the idea of Managing by Asking Around (MBAA).

The MBAA tour I was taking was not physical (walking around) but intellectual (thinking and asking around) driven by the Socratic Management Paradigm.

I hope you find this book a blueprint for Management by Asking Around!

Mixing MBWA and MBAA

I would be cautious about mixing MBWA and MBAA. If you throw a bunch of questions at people whenever you visit them in their world, they will soon not welcome your ostensibly personal touch.

CHAPTER SUMMARY

- Management by Walking Around (MBWA) is a physical tour of your world.
- Management by Asking Around (MBAA) is an intellectual tour of your world, driven by the Socratic Management Paradigm.
- Both MBAA and MBWA are important to becoming a great manager.
- Be cautious about mixing MBWA and MBAA.

SUMMARY AND AFTERWORD

This book is about defining a meta-process, a model, a paradigm, a way of thinking, for and about management.

If you don't have a paradigm for management, you're doing improv management, which is sometimes entertaining, but fundamentally unguided. And improv management is scary for everyone. So, you need a paradigm for how you are going to manage.

My Socratic Management Paradigm has two parts – asking questions of others and asking questions of yourself.

• For *most of your managerial world*, in managing others, you need to:

    ✓ know the right questions,

    ✓ segue to the right follow-on questions,

    ✓ recognize wrong answers, and

    ✓ know where to find the right answers.

- For some *small part of your managerial world*, in managing others, you need to:
  - ✓ Know in which small part of your managerial world you must be an expert, and
  - ✓ For that small percentage of your managerial world, know both the right questions and the right answers.
- To manage yourself, you need to ask yourself:
  - ✓ Am I asking questions well?
  - ✓ Am I courageous and honest?
  - ✓ Am I principled?
  - ✓ Am I listening and talking to myself?
  - ✓ Am I connecting leadership and management?
  - ✓ Am I simplifying?
- When you ask yourself, you likely already know the answer.

I've written this book in a unique voice, born of a combination of twenty-two years as a Naval Officer, and twenty-three years as a civilian consultant, teacher, and CEO.

The examples herein are to give you real-world illustrations from my experiences. I hope that you can translate the lessons into your reality.

This has been a labor of love and passion. I hope this book makes a difference in the lives of those who have taken on the difficult and yet incredibly rewarding mantle of management.

Good luck and Godspeed.

ACKNOWLEDGMENTS

I want to first acknowledge and honor my wife of thirty-seven years, partner for forty-two years, and friend of forty-seven years, Catherine Moore, MD. A practicing psychiatrist for more than a third of a century, she has taught me so much about myself and the human mind.

There were many people who read subsequent drafts of this book, but I want to express my special thanks to the readers of the first drafts: James and Carmen Beaubeaux, Leslie Bruce, Jeff Fischbeck, Jim Groen, and Jim Hay.

My thanks to my mentor, Karla Olson, who guided me through the process of getting this manuscript to print. The fabulous design team of Alan Dino Hebel and Ian Koviak at theBookDesigners made my words look great.

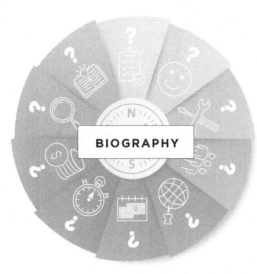

BIOGRAPHY

Tom Gehring was born in Cologne, Germany, in 1953, and lived in Germany, France, India, and the United States before graduating from Rice University with a double major in Electrical Engineering and Applied Mathematics in 1976.

He served for twenty-two years in the United States Navy, almost all of it at sea in nuclear submarines.

After retiring from active duty in 1998, he spent three years at Booz|Allen|Hamilton as a senior strategic consultant.

From 2001 until his retirement in 2015 he was the CEO of the San Diego County Medical Society (SDCMS), representing more than 8,000 physicians in the eighth-largest city in the United States.

He now teaches and writes on leadership and management.

BIBLIOGRAPHY

Adams, Scott. *Dogbert's Top Secret Management Handbook.*

Ambrose, Stephen. *Undaunted Courage.*

Buckingham, Marcus. *First Break All The Rules.*

Cheyfitz, Kris. *Thinking Inside the Box.*

Gehring, Tom. *7 Roles Great Leaders Don't Delegate.*

Logan, Dave. *Tribal Leadership.*

Madea, John. *The Laws of Simplicity.*

Oliver, Dave. *Against the Tide.*

Pfeffer, Jeffrey. *Managing with Power.*

Sinek, Simon. *Start With Why.*

Sontag, Sherry, and Christopher Drew. *Blind Man's Bluff.*

Stone, Douglas. *Difficult Conversations – How to Discuss What Matters Most.*

Useem, Michael. *Leading Up.*

Wilson, Paul, Larry Dell, and Gaylord Anderson. *Root Cause Analysis.*

APPENDIX 1: PRETTY GOOD RULES AND QUESTIONS FOR MANAGERS

- KISS: Keep It Simple and Short.
- It is better to sweat in peace than bleed in war. — *Winston Churchill*
- Nothing hard is ever easy.[28]
- Knowing the right thing to do is easy. Doing the right thing is hard. — *General Norman Schwarzkopf*
- Why? Why? Why? Why? Why? Why? — *Admiral Hyman Rickover*
- Ninety percent of effective management is knowing the right question to ask—and the wrong answer.
- Improvise, adapt, and overcome. — *Clint Eastwood in the movie* Heartbreak Ridge.

---

28   And the wags would argue that sometimes, often, nothing easy is ever easy!

- You can't fix what ain't broke—but you can watch it very carefully.
- Life is tough, but it's tougher if you're stupid. — *John Wayne in the movie* The Sands of Iwo Jima
- You can't fix stupid.
- You do what you can, where you're at, with what you have. — *President Theodore Roosevelt*
- Don't stop in the middle of the freeway.
- No plan ever survives first contact with the enemy or with reality. — *Field Marshal Helmuth von Moltke*
- Good judgment comes from experience, and experience comes from poor judgment.
- The buck stops here. —*President Harry Truman*
- In a tough spot, ask out loud, in public, "What's the right thing to do here?"
- In a tough spot, ask out loud, in public, "Is this legal, ethical, and moral?"
- Never argue with an idiot in public—you won't win the argument, and those watching won't be able to tell the difference between you and the idiot.
- What just didn't happen here?
- Never wrestle with a pig; the pig likes it, and you're going to get dirty.
- Plans are nothing, planning is everything. —*General Dwight D. Eisenhower*

APPENDIX 2: ALL 11 QUESTIONS AND FOLLOW-ON QUESTIONS

To define the problem, ask:

1. **What is the problem we are trying to solve?**
   Can everyone understand the problem statement?
   Is the problem statement compelling?
   Have all the customers and stakeholders concurred?
   Has success been defined?

2. **Why are we solving this problem?**
   Why is solving this problem important?
   How is solving this problem connected to the fundamental goals of the organization?
   What's in it for me?
   Who really cares about solving this problem?
   What is the return on investment (ROI) for solving this problem?

3. **For whom are we solving this problem?**

   Who are the customers?

   Are there multiple voices from a "single" customer?

   Who are the stakeholders?

   Have all the stakeholders opined?

   Are they customers or are they really stakeholders?

   Have you followed the money?

To generate a solution, ask:

4. **How are we going to solve this problem?**

   Has this problem been solved before?

   What do history and best practices tell us?

   How granular do you want to be?

   What parts/tools/personnel do you need?

   What are you personally going to do?

   What are the interdependencies?

   Have we "Red Teamed" this solution?

   What "Black Swans" have we identified?

   Have we done a pre-mortem?

   What's the definition of success?

   Do we need to change the definition of success?

5. **Who will do what?**

   Is one person assigned responsibility for each task?

   Is the task matched to the person?

   Do people have enough bandwidth and/or priority to
   achieve assigned tasks?

   Have you matched passion to task?

   How's it going for you?

   How's it going for your team?

   What tasks are you outsourcing?

6. **Where are we doing what?**

    Why are we doing that there?

    How will weather affect our tasks?

    How will the politics of a given location impact our tasks?

    What can be done virtually?

7. **When are we doing what?**

    When are we doing the really hard stuff?

    How much rest has your team had?

    Can I see the master calendar?

    What is going on outside the organization?

    What about environmental factors that are time related?

    What are the key events in the next major time frame?

8. **How long will it take?**

    How do you know?

    What are the assumptions underlying this time estimate?

    What do history and best practices tell us?

    Can I see the timeline?

    What one tool are we using to track the timeline?

    What are the likely causes of schedule slip?

    What specific steps will you take to control schedule slip?

    When is the next schedule review meeting?

    What happens if the schedule slips?

9. **How much will it cost?**

   How do you know how much it will cost?

   What are the underlying assumptions to the cost estimate?

   What do history and best practices tell us?

   Can I see the budget?

   What one tool are we using to track budget?

   What are the likely causes of overbudget?

   What specific steps will you take to control overbudget?

   When is the next budget review meeting?

   What happens if the budget goes into the red?

   Where are the contingency budget lines?

To implement the solution, ask:

10. **How are we doing on the plan?**

    We do have a plan, right?

    When is our next project status meeting?

    What system are we using to track progress?

    Is everyone actually using the designated system?

    Is the data being updated?

    What's our goal?

    Are we there yet?

    Have you gone and looked?

    Have you positioned yourself where you can see clearly?

    Have you asked, "Why? Why? Why? Why? Why?" until you get to bedrock causality?

    How will you correct this problem?

    Can you "Improvise, Adapt, and Overcome?"

11. **How are we learning and improving?**

    Is there a lesson in this failure?

    How are we getting better?

    How do we promulgate lessons learned?

    How do we spread the intellectual wealth?

INDEX

Made in the USA
Coppell, TX
31 August 2020